THE
PROFESSIONAL
PRACTICES
FRAMEWORK

The IIA Research
Foundation

Disclosure

The IIA publishes this document for informational and educational purposes. This document is intended to provide information, but is not a substitute for legal or accounting advice. The IIA does not provide such advice and makes no warranty as to any legal or accounting results through its publication of this document. When legal or accounting issues arise, professional assistance should be sought and retained.

The Professional Practices Framework for Internal Auditing (PPF) was designed by The IIA Board of Directors' Guidance Task Force to appropriately organize the full range of existing and developing practice guidance for the profession. Based on the definition of internal auditing, the PPF comprises Ethics and *Standards,* Practice Advisories, and Development and Practice Aids, and paves the way to world-class internal auditing. This guidance fits into the Framework under the heading Development and Practice Aids.

The mission of The IIA Research Foundation (IIARF) is to be the global leader in sponsoring, disseminating, and promoting research and knowledge resources to enhance the development and effectiveness of the internal auditing profession.

The Institute of Internal Auditors
Global Practices Center
247 Maitland Avenue
Altamonte Springs, FL 32701-4201 USA
Phone: +1-407-937-1362
FAX: +1-407-937-1101
E-mail: standards@theiia.org

ISBN 0-89413-558-9
04643   01/05
First Printing
05507   08/05
Second Printing

CONTENTS

Practice Advisories
Attribute Standards

Topical Index to Practice Advisories
Audit Charter

Assumption of Non-audit Duties

Assurance

Board and Senior Management Reporting

Governance

Independence and Objectivity

Internal Control

Outsourcing or Co-sourcing

PREFACE

In June 1999, the Board of Directors of The Institute of Internal Auditors (IIA) voted to approve a new definition of internal auditing and a new Professional Practices Framework (PPF). Both were based on the recommendations of the Guidance Task Force, a special committee of The IIA charged with examining the adequacy of current standards and guidance for the practice of internal auditing. The Task Force concluded that a significant gap existed between available guidance and current practice and that a new framework was needed to carry the profession into the 21st century. In order to meet this goal, The IIA developed the PPF. Following an exposure draft circulated in January 2003, The IIA's Internal Auditing Standards Board (IASB) just released the second major revision to the *International Standards for the Professional Practice of Internal Auditing (Standards)* since they were first issued about a quarter of a century ago. The Professional Issues Committee has also carried out an extensive maintenance review of the PPF. The revised *Standards,* Practice Advisories, and guidance are extremely significant to our global profession and are a part of the process to develop a new PPF. The new *Standards* became mandatory guidance for all IIA members and Certified Internal Auditors (CIAs) on January 1, 2004.

In general, a framework provides a structural blueprint of how a body of knowledge and guidance fit together. As a coherent system, it facilitates consistent development, interpretation, and application of concepts, methodologies, and techniques useful to a discipline or profession. Specifically, the purpose of the PPF is to organize the full range of internal audit guidance in a manner that is readily accessible on a timely basis. By encompassing current internal audit practice as well as allowing for future expansion, the PPF is intended to assist practitioners throughout the world in being responsive to the expanding market for high quality internal audit services.

Internal auditing is an independent, objective assurance and consulting activity designed to add value and improve an organization's operations. It helps an organization accomplish its objectives by bringing a systematic, disciplined approach to evaluate and improve the effectiveness of risk management, control, and governance processes.

Throughout the world, internal auditing is performed in diverse environments and within organizations that vary in purpose, size, and structure. In addition, the laws and customs within various countries differ from one another. These differences may affect the practice of internal auditing in each environment. The implementation of the PPF, therefore, will be governed by the environment in which the internal audit activity carries out its assigned responsibilities. No information contained within the PPF should be construed in a manner that conflicts with applicable laws or regulations. If a situation arises where information contained within the PPF may be in conflict with legislation or regulation, internal auditors are encouraged to contact The IIA or legal counsel for further guidance.

The PPF consists of three categories of guidance: *Standards* and Ethics, Practice Advisories, and Development and Practice Aids. The first category (Mandatory Guidance) consists of core materials: the Code of Ethics and the *Standards*. All mandatory guidance has been submitted for review by the profession through the exposure draft process and is considered to be essential for the professional practice of internal auditing. Other elements of the PPF are linked to these *Standards*.

The purpose of The IIA's Code of Ethics is to promote an ethical culture in the profession of internal auditing. A code of ethics is necessary and appropriate for the profession of internal auditing, founded as it is on the trust placed in its objective assurance about risk management, control, and governance.

Standards, as described within the PPF, are the criteria by which the operations of an internal audit department are evaluated and measured. They are intended to represent the practice of internal auditing as it should be. The *Standards* are meant to serve the entire profession of internal auditing, in all types of organizations where internal auditors are found. Within the new PPF, the Guidance Task Force called for the development of three sets of standards: Attribute, Performance, and Implementation Standards. The Attribute Standards address the attributes of organizations and individuals performing internal audit services. The Performance Standards describe the nature of internal audit services and provide quality criteria against which the performance of these services can be measured. The Attribute and Performance Standards apply to all internal audit services. The Implementation Standards expand upon the Attribute and Performance Standards, providing guidance applicable in specific types of engagements. These standards ultimately may deal with industry-specific, regional, or specialty types of audit services.

Compliance with the concepts enunciated in the mandatory guidance is essential before the responsibilities of internal auditors can be met. As stated in the Code of Ethics, internal auditors shall perform internal audit services in accordance with the *Standards*. All members of The IIA and all CIAs agree to abide by the *Standards* and Code of Ethics, and this guidance is intended to be applicable to all members of the internal audit profession, whether or not they are members of The IIA.

To be widely applicable, mandatory guidance must necessarily be somewhat generic in nature. Therefore, the PPF includes two additional categories of guidance. Guidance in the second category, the Practice Advisories (formerly known as Guidelines) are strongly recommended and endorsed by The IIA. Although not mandatory, Practice Advisories represent best practices endorsed by The IIA as ways to implement the *Standards*. In part, Practice Advisories may help to interpret the *Standards* or to apply them in specific internal audit environments. Many Practice Advisories are applicable to all internal auditors, while others may be developed to meet the needs of internal auditors in a specific industry, audit specialty, or geographic area. All Practice Advisories are submitted to a formal review process by The IIA's Professional Issues Committee or other group designated by the Guidance Planning Committee.

The third category of guidance (Development and Practice Aids) includes a variety of materials that are developed and/or endorsed by The IIA. This category includes research studies, books, seminars, conferences, and other products and services related to the professional practice of internal auditing that do not meet the criteria for inclusion in mandatory guidance or Practice Advisories. Development and practice aids can help to implement the guidance offered in the Code of Ethics, *Standards*, and Practice Advisories. Development and practice aids provide internal audit practitioners with the views of various experts on techniques and processes related to the professional practice of internal auditing.

During the coming years, internal auditors can help to ensure that the PPF will continue to grow more robust through their active involvement in guidance development. All interested parties are invited to provide comments and suggestions about any aspect of the PPF. For professional guidance, comments, and suggestions, send an e-mail to issues@theiia.org. To find out about coming additions to the PPF, internal auditors are encouraged to monitor the Guidance Development page at http://www.theiia.org.

ACKNOWLEDGMENTS

The Institute of Internal Auditors (IIA) is grateful to those government agencies, professional organizations, internal and external auditors, and members of management, boards of directors, and academe who provided guidance and assistance in the development and interpretation of the *International Standards for the Professional Practice of Internal Auditing (Standards)*. The IIA is deeply indebted to those individuals who served on the Internal Auditing Standards Board, Professional Issues Committee, and other international committees through the years.

DEFINITION OF INTERNAL AUDITING

Internal auditing is an independent, objective assurance and consulting activity designed to add value and improve an organization's operations. It helps an organization accomplish its objectives by bringing a systematic, disciplined approach to evaluate and improve the effectiveness of risk management, control, and governance processes.

CODE OF ETHICS

Introduction

The purpose of The Institute's Code of Ethics is to promote an ethical culture in the profession of internal auditing.

> *Internal auditing is an independent, objective assurance and consulting activity designed to add value and improve an organization's operations. It helps an organization accomplish its objectives by bringing a systematic, disciplined approach to evaluate and improve the effectiveness of risk management, control, and governance processes.*

A code of ethics is necessary and appropriate for the profession of internal auditing, founded as it is on the trust placed in its objective assurance about risk management, control, and governance. The Institute's Code of Ethics extends beyond the definition of internal auditing to include two essential components:

1. Principles that are relevant to the profession and practice of internal auditing;
2. Rules of Conduct that describe behavior norms expected of internal auditors. These rules are an aid to interpreting the Principles into practical applications and are intended to guide the ethical conduct of internal auditors.

The Code of Ethics together with The Institute's Professional Practices Framework and other relevant Institute pronouncements provide guidance to internal auditors serving others. "Internal auditors" refers to Institute members, recipients of or candidates for IIA professional certifications, and those who provide internal auditing services within the definition of internal auditing.

Applicability and Enforcement

This Code of Ethics applies to both individuals and entities that provide internal auditing services.

For Institute members and recipients of or candidates for IIA professional certifications, breaches of the Code of Ethics will be evaluated and administered according to The Institute's Bylaws and Administrative Guidelines. The fact that a particular conduct is not mentioned in the Rules of Conduct does not prevent it from being unacceptable or discreditable, and, therefore, the member, certification holder, or candidate can be liable for disciplinary action.

Principles

Internal auditors are expected to apply and uphold the following principles:

Integrity

The integrity of internal auditors establishes trust and thus provides the basis for reliance on their judgment.

Objectivity

Internal auditors exhibit the highest level of professional objectivity in gathering, evaluating, and communicating information about the activity or process being examined. Internal auditors make a balanced assessment of all the relevant circumstances and are not unduly influenced by their own interests or by others in forming judgments.

Confidentiality

Internal auditors respect the value and ownership of information they receive and do not disclose information without appropriate authority unless there is a legal or professional obligation to do so.

Competency

Internal auditors apply the knowledge, skills, and experience needed in the performance of internal auditing services.

Rules of Conduct

1. **Integrity**
   Internal auditors:

   1.1. Shall perform their work with honesty, diligence, and responsibility.
   1.2. Shall observe the law and make disclosures expected by the law and the profession.
   1.3. Shall not knowingly be a party to any illegal activity, or engage in acts that are discreditable to the profession of internal auditing or to the organization.
   1.4. Shall respect and contribute to the legitimate and ethical objectives of the organization.

2. **Objectivity**
   Internal auditors:

   2.1. Shall not participate in any activity or relationship that may impair or be presumed to impair their unbiased assessment. This participation includes those activities or relationships that may be in conflict with the interests of the organization.

2.2. Shall not accept anything that may impair or be presumed to impair their professional judgment.

2.3. Shall disclose all material facts known to them that, if not disclosed, may distort the reporting of activities under review.

3. Confidentiality
Internal auditors:

3.1 Shall be prudent in the use and protection of information acquired in the course of their duties.

3.2 Shall not use information for any personal gain or in any manner that would be contrary to the law or detrimental to the legitimate and ethical objectives of the organization.

4. Competency
Internal auditors:

4.1. Shall engage only in those services for which they have the necessary knowledge, skills, and experience.

4.2 Shall perform internal auditing services in accordance with the *International Standards for the Professional Practice of Internal Auditing.*

4.3 Shall continually improve their proficiency and the effectiveness and quality of their services.

INTERNATIONAL STANDARDS FOR THE PROFESSIONAL PRACTICE OF INTERNAL AUDITING

INTRODUCTION

Internal audit activities are performed in diverse legal and cultural environments; within organizations that vary in purpose, size, complexity, and structure; and by persons within or outside the organization. While differences may affect the practice of internal auditing in each environment, compliance with the *International Standards for the Professional Practice of Internal Auditing (Standards)* is essential if the responsibilities of internal auditors are to be met. If internal auditors are prohibited by laws or regulations from complying with certain parts of the *Standards*, they should comply with all other parts of the *Standards* and make appropriate disclosures.

Assurance services involve the internal auditor's objective assessment of evidence to provide an independent opinion or conclusions regarding a process, system, or other subject matter. The nature and scope of the assurance engagement are determined by the internal auditor. There are generally three parties involved in assurance services: (1) the person or group directly involved with the process, system, or other subject matter — the process owner, (2) the person or group making the assessment — the internal auditor, and (3) the person or group using the assessment — the user.

Consulting services are advisory in nature, and are generally performed at the specific request of an engagement client. The nature and scope of the consulting engagement are subject to agreement with the engagement client. Consulting services generally involve two parties: (1) the person or group offering the advice — the internal auditor, and (2) the person or group seeking and receiving the advice — the engagement client. When performing consulting services the internal auditor should maintain objectivity and not assume management responsibility.

The purpose of the *Standards* is to:

1. Delineate basic principles that represent the practice of internal auditing as it should be.
2. Provide a framework for performing and promoting a broad range of valuc-added internal audit activities.
3. Establish the basis for the evaluation of internal audit performance.
4. Foster improved organizational processes and operations.

The *Standards* consist of Attribute Standards, Performance Standards, and Implementation Standards. The Attribute Standards address the characteristics of organizations and parties performing internal audit activities. The Performance Standards describe the nature of internal audit activities and provide quality criteria against which the performance of these services can be evaluated. While the Attribute and Performance Standards apply to all internal audit services, the Implementation Standards apply to specific types of engagements.

There is one set of Attribute and Performance Standards; however, there are multiple sets of Implementation Standards: a set for each of the major types of internal audit activity. The Implementation Standards have been established for assurance (A) and consulting (C) activities.

The *Standards* are part of the Professional Practices Framework. The Professional Practices Framework includes the Definition of Internal Auditing, the Code of Ethics, the *Standards*, and other guidance. Guidance regarding how the *Standards* might be applied is included in Practice Advisories that are issued by the Professional Issues Committee.

The *Standards* employ terms that have been given specific meanings that are included in the Glossary.

The development and issuance of the *Standards* is an ongoing process. The Internal Auditing Standards Board engages in extensive consultation and discussion prior to the issuance of the *Standards*. This includes worldwide solicitation for public comment through the exposure draft process.

All exposure drafts are posted on The IIA's Web site as well as being distributed to all IIA affiliates. Suggestions and comments regarding the *Standards* can be sent to:

The Institute of Internal Auditors
Global Practices Center,
Professional Practices Group
247 Maitland Avenue
Altamonte Springs, FL 32701-4201, USA
E-mail: standards@theiia.org
Web: http://www.theiia.org

The latest additions and amendments to the *Standards* became effective January 1, 2004.

ATTRIBUTE STANDARDS

1000 – Purpose, Authority, and Responsibility
The purpose, authority, and responsibility of the internal audit activity should be formally defined in a charter, consistent with the *Standards*, and approved by the board.

> **1000.A1** – The nature of assurance services provided to the organization should be defined in the audit charter. If assurances are to be provided to parties outside the organization, the nature of these assurances should also be defined in the charter.

> **1000.C1** – The nature of consulting services should be defined in the audit charter.

1100 – Independence and Objectivity
The internal audit activity should be independent, and internal auditors should be objective in performing their work.

1110 – Organizational Independence
The chief audit executive should report to a level within the organization that allows the internal audit activity to fulfill its responsibilities.

> **1110.A1** – The internal audit activity should be free from interference in determining the scope of internal auditing, performing work, and communicating results.

1120 – Individual Objectivity
Internal auditors should have an impartial, unbiased attitude and avoid conflicts of interest.

1130 – Impairments to Independence or Objectivity

If independence or objectivity is impaired in fact or appearance, the details of the impairment should be disclosed to appropriate parties. The nature of the disclosure will depend upon the impairment.

> **1130.A1** – Internal auditors should refrain from assessing specific operations for which they were previously responsible. Objectivity is presumed to be impaired if an internal auditor provides assurance services for an activity for which the internal auditor had responsibility within the previous year.

> **1130.A2** – Assurance engagements for functions over which the chief audit executive has responsibility should be overseen by a party outside the internal audit activity.

> **1130.C1** – Internal auditors may provide consulting services relating to operations for which they had previous responsibilities.

> **1130.C2** – If internal auditors have potential impairments to independence or objectivity relating to proposed consulting services, disclosure should be made to the engagement client prior to accepting the engagement.

1200 – Proficiency and Due Professional Care

Engagements should be performed with proficiency and due professional care.

1210 – Proficiency

Internal auditors should possess the knowledge, skills, and other competencies needed to perform their individual responsibilities. The internal audit activity collectively should possess or obtain the knowledge, skills, and other competencies needed to perform its responsibilities.

1210.A1 – The chief audit executive should obtain competent advice and assistance if the internal audit staff lacks the knowledge, skills, or other competencies needed to perform all or part of the engagement.

1210.A2 – The internal auditor should have sufficient knowledge to identify the indicators of fraud but is not expected to have the expertise of a person whose primary responsibility is detecting and investigating fraud.

1210.A3 – Internal auditors should have knowledge of key information technology risks and controls and available technology-based audit techniques to perform their assigned work. However, not all internal auditors are expected to have the expertise of an internal auditor whose primary responsibility is information technology auditing.

1210.C1 – The chief audit executive should decline the consulting engagement or obtain competent advice and assistance if the internal audit staff lacks the knowledge, skills, or other competencies needed to perform all or part of the engagement.

1220 – Due Professional Care
Internal auditors should apply the care and skill expected of a reasonably prudent and competent internal auditor. Due professional care does not imply infallibility.

1220.A1 – The internal auditor should exercise due professional care by considering the:
- Extent of work needed to achieve the engagement's objectives.

- Relative complexity, materiality, or significance of matters to which assurance procedures are applied.
- Adequacy and effectiveness of risk management, control, and governance processes.
- Probability of significant errors, irregularities, or noncompliance.
- Cost of assurance in relation to potential benefits.

1220.A2 – In exercising due professional care the internal auditor should consider the use of computer-assisted audit tools and other data analysis techniques.

1220.A3 – The internal auditor should be alert to the significant risks that might affect objectives, operations, or resources. However, assurance procedures alone, even when performed with due professional care, do not guarantee that all significant risks will be identified.

1220.C1 – The internal auditor should exercise due professional care during a consulting engagement by considering the:
- Needs and expectations of clients, including the nature, timing, and communication of engagement results.
- Relative complexity and extent of work needed to achieve the engagement's objectives.
- Cost of the consulting engagement in relation to potential benefits.

1230 – Continuing Professional Development
Internal auditors should enhance their knowledge, skills, and other competencies through continuing professional development.

1300 – Quality Assurance and Improvement Program

The chief audit executive should develop and maintain a quality assurance and improvement program that covers all aspects of the internal audit activity and continuously monitors its effectiveness. This program includes periodic internal and external quality assessments and ongoing internal monitoring. Each part of the program should be designed to help the internal auditing activity add value and improve the organization's operations and to provide assurance that the internal audit activity is in conformity with the *Standards* and the Code of Ethics.

1310 – Quality Program Assessments

The internal audit activity should adopt a process to monitor and assess the overall effectiveness of the quality program. The process should include both internal and external assessments.

1311 – Internal Assessments

Internal assessments should include:
- Ongoing reviews of the performance of the internal audit activity; and
- Periodic reviews performed through self-assessment or by other persons within the organization, with knowledge of internal audit practices and the *Standards*.

1312 – External Assessments

External assessments, such as quality assurance reviews, should be conducted at least once every five years by a qualified, independent reviewer or review team from outside the organization.

1320 – Reporting on the Quality Program

The chief audit executive should communicate the results of external assessments to the board.

1330 – Use of "Conducted in Accordance with the *Standards*"

Internal auditors are encouraged to report that their activities are "conducted in accordance with the *International Standards for the Professional Practice of Internal Auditing*." However, internal auditors may use the statement only if assessments of the quality improvement program demonstrate that the internal audit activity is in compliance with the *Standards*.

1340 – Disclosure of Noncompliance

Although the internal audit activity should achieve full compliance with the *Standards* and internal auditors with the Code of Ethics, there may be instances in which full compliance is not achieved. When noncompliance impacts the overall scope or operation of the internal audit activity, disclosure should be made to senior management and the board.

PERFORMANCE STANDARDS

2000 – Managing the Internal Audit Activity
The chief audit executive should effectively manage the internal audit activity to ensure it adds value to the organization.

2010 – Planning
The chief audit executive should establish risk-based plans to determine the priorities of the internal audit activity, consistent with the organization's goals.

2010.A1 – The internal audit activity's plan of engagements should be based on a risk assessment, undertaken at least annually. The input of senior management and the board should be considered in this process.

2010.C1 – The chief audit executive should consider accepting proposed consulting engagements based on the engagement's potential to improve management of risks, add value, and improve the organization's operations. Those engagements that have been accepted should be included in the plan.

2020 – Communication and Approval
The chief audit executive should communicate the internal audit activity's plans and resource requirements, including significant interim changes, to senior management and to the board for review and approval. The chief audit executive should also communicate the impact of resource limitations.

2030 – Resource Management
The chief audit executive should ensure that internal audit resources are appropriate, sufficient, and effectively deployed to achieve the approved plan.

2040 – Policies and Procedures
The chief audit executive should establish policies and procedures to guide the internal audit activity.

2050 – Coordination
The chief audit executive should share information and coordinate activities with other internal and external providers of relevant assurance and consulting services to ensure proper coverage and minimize duplication of efforts.

2060 – Reporting to the Board and Senior Management
The chief audit executive should report periodically to the board and senior management on the internal audit activity's purpose, authority, responsibility, and performance relative to its plan. Reporting should also include significant risk exposures and control issues, corporate governance issues, and other matters needed or requested by the board and senior management.

2100 – Nature of Work
The internal audit activity should evaluate and contribute to the improvement of risk management, control, and governance processes using a systematic and disciplined approach.

2110 – Risk Management
The internal audit activity should assist the organization by identifying and evaluating significant exposures to risk and contributing to the improvement of risk management and control systems.

2110.A1 – The internal audit activity should monitor and evaluate the effectiveness of the organization's risk management system.

2110.A2 – The internal audit activity should evaluate risk exposures relating to the organization's governance, operations, and information systems regarding the:
- Reliability and integrity of financial and operational information.
- Effectiveness and efficiency of operations.
- Safeguarding of assets.
- Compliance with laws, regulations, and contracts.

2110.C1 – During consulting engagements, internal auditors should address risk consistent with the engagement's objectives and be alert to the existence of other significant risks.

2110.C2 – Internal auditors should incorporate knowledge of risks gained from consulting engagements into the process of identifying and evaluating significant risk exposures of the organization.

2120 – Control
The internal audit activity should assist the organization in maintaining effective controls by evaluating their effectiveness and efficiency and by promoting continuous improvement.

2120.A1 – Based on the results of the risk assessment, the internal audit activity should evaluate the adequacy and effectiveness of controls encompassing the organization's governance, operations, and information systems. This should include:
- Reliability and integrity of financial and operational information.

- Effectiveness and efficiency of operations.
- Safeguarding of assets.
- Compliance with laws, regulations, and contracts.

2120.A2 – Internal auditors should ascertain the extent to which operating and program goals and objectives have been established and conform to those of the organization.

2120.A3 – Internal auditors should review operations and programs to ascertain the extent to which results are consistent with established goals and objectives to determine whether operations and programs are being implemented or performed as intended.

2120.A4 – Adequate criteria are needed to evaluate controls. Internal auditors should ascertain the extent to which management has established adequate criteria to determine whether objectives and goals have been accomplished. If adequate, internal auditors should use such criteria in their evaluation. If inadequate, internal auditors should work with management to develop appropriate evaluation criteria.

2120.C1 – During consulting engagements, internal auditors should address controls consistent with the engagement's objectives and be alert to the existence of any significant control weaknesses.

2120.C2 – Internal auditors should incorporate knowledge of controls gained from consulting engagements into the process of identifying and evaluating significant risk exposures of the organization.

2130 – Governance

The internal audit activity should assess and make appropriate reeommendations for improving the governance process in its accomplishment of the following objectives:

- Promoting appropriate ethics and values within the organization.
- Ensuring effective organizational performance management and accountability.
- Effectively communicating risk and control information to appropriate areas of the organization.
- Effectively coordinating the activities of and communicating information among the board, external and internal auditors, and management.

2130.A1 – The internal audit activity should evaluate the design, implementation, and effectiveness of the organization's ethics-related objectives, programs, and activities.

2130.C1 – Consulting engagement objectives should be consistent with the overall values and goals of the organization.

2200 – Engagement Planning

Internal auditors should develop and record a plan for each engagement, including the scope, objectives, timing, and resource allocations.

2201 – Planning Considerations

In planning the engagement, internal auditors should consider:

- The objectives of the activity being reviewed and the means by which the activity controls its performance.
- The significant risks to the activity, its objectives, resources, and operations and the means by which the potential impact of risk is kept to an acceptable level.

- The adequacy and effectiveness of the activity's risk management and control systems compared to a relevant control framework or model.
- The opportunities for making significant improvements to the activity's risk management and control systems.

2201.A1 – When planning an engagement for parties outside the organization, internal auditors should establish a written understanding with them about objectives, scope, respective responsibilities, and other expectations, including restrictions on distribution of the results of the engagement and access to engagement records.

2201.C1 – Internal auditors should establish an understanding with consulting engagement clients about objectives, scope, respective responsibilities, and other client expectations. For significant engagements, this understanding should be documented.

2210 – Engagement Objectives
Objectives should be established for each engagement.

2210.A1 – Internal auditors should conduct a preliminary assessment of the risks relevant to the activity under review. Engagement objectives should reflect the results of this assessment.

2210.A2 – The internal auditor should consider the probability of significant errors, irregularities, noncompliance, and other exposures when developing the engagement objectives.

2210.C1 – Consulting engagement objectives should address risks, controls, and governance processes to the extent agreed upon with the client.

2220 – Engagement Scope

The established scope should be sufficient to satisfy the objectives of the engagement.

2220.A1 – The scope of the engagement should include consideration of relevant systems, records, personnel, and physical properties, including those under the control of third parties.

2220.A2 – If significant consulting opportunities arise during an assurance engagement, a specific written understanding as to the objectives, scope, respective responsibilities, and other expectations should be reached and the results of the consulting engagement communicated in accordance with consulting standards.

2220.C1 – In performing consulting engagements, internal auditors should ensure that the scope of the engagement is sufficient to address the agreed-upon objectives. If internal auditors develop reservations about the scope during the engagement, these reservations should be discussed with the client to determine whether to continue with the engagement.

2230 – Engagement Resource Allocation

Internal auditors should determine appropriate resources to achieve engagement objectives. Staffing should be based on an evaluation of the nature and complexity of each engagement, time constraints, and available resources.

2240 – Engagement Work Program

Internal auditors should develop work programs that achieve the engagement objectives. These work programs should be recorded.

2240.A1 – Work programs should establish the procedures for identifying, analyzing, evaluating, and recording information during the engagement. The work program should be approved prior to its implementation, and any adjustments approved promptly.

2240.C1 – Work programs for consulting engagements may vary in form and content depending upon the nature of the engagement.

2300 – Performing the Engagement

Internal auditors should identify, analyze, evaluate, and record sufficient information to achieve the engagement's objectives.

2310 – Identifying Information

Internal auditors should identify sufficient, reliable, relevant, and useful information to achieve the engagement's objectives.

2320 – Analysis and Evaluation

Internal auditors should base conclusions and engagement results on appropriate analyses and evaluations.

2330 – Recording Information

Internal auditors should record relevant information to support the conclusions and engagement results.

2330.A1 – The chief audit executive should control access to engagement records. The chief audit executive should obtain the approval of senior management and/or legal counsel prior to releasing such records to external parties, as appropriate.

2330.A2 – The chief audit executive should develop retention requirements for engagement records. These retention requirements should be consistent with the organization's guidelines and any pertinent regulatory or other requirements.

2330.C1 – The chief audit executive should develop policies governing the custody and retention of engagement records, as well as their release to internal and external parties. These policies should be consistent with the organization's guidelines and any pertinent regulatory or other requirements.

2340 – Engagement Supervision
Engagements should be properly supervised to ensure objectives are achieved, quality is assured, and staff is developed.

2400 – Communicating Results
Internal auditors should communicate the engagement results.

2410 – Criteria for Communicating
Communications should include the engagement's objectives and scope as well as applicable conclusions, recommendations, and action plans.

2410.A1 – Final communication of engagement results should, where appropriate, contain the internal auditor's overall opinion and or conclusions.

2410.A2 – Internal auditors are encouraged to acknowledge satisfactory performance in engagement communications.

2410.A3 – When releasing engagement results to parties outside the organization, the communication should include limitations on distribution and use of the results.

2410.C1 – Communication of the progress and results of consulting engagements will vary in form and content depending upon the nature of the engagement and the needs of the client.

2420 – Quality of Communications
Communications should be accurate, objective, clear, concise, constructive, complete, and timely.

2421 – Errors and Omissions
If a final communication contains a significant error or omission, the chief audit executive should communicate corrected information to all parties who received the original communication.

2430 – Engagement Disclosure of Noncompliance with the *Standards*
When noncompliance with the *Standards* impacts a specific engagement, communication of the results should disclose the:
- *Standard(s)* with which full compliance was not achieved,
- Reason(s) for noncompliance, and
- Impact of noncompliance on the engagement.

2440 – Disseminating Results
The chief audit executive should communicate results to the appropriate parties.

2440.A1 – The chief audit executive is responsible for communicating the final results to parties who can ensure that the results are given due consideration.

2440.A2 – If not otherwise mandated by legal, statutory, or regulatory requirements, prior to releasing results to parties outside the organization, the chief audit executive should:

- Assess the potential risk to the organization.
- Consult with senior management and/or legal counsel as appropriate.
- Control dissemination by restricting the use of the results.

2440.C1 – The chief audit executive is responsible for communicating the final results of consulting engagements to clients.

2440.C2 – During consulting engagements, risk management, control, and governance issues may be identified. Whenever these issues are significant to the organization, they should be communicated to senior management and the board.

2500 – Monitoring Progress
The chief audit executive should establish and maintain a system to monitor the disposition of results communicated to management.

2500.A1 – The chief audit executive should establish a followup process to monitor and ensure that management actions have been effectively implemented or that senior management has accepted the risk of not taking action.

2500.C1 – The internal audit activity should monitor the disposition of results of consulting engagements to the extent agreed upon with the client.

2600 – Resolution of Management's Acceptance of Risks
When the chief audit executive believes that senior management has accepted a level of residual risk that may be unacceptable to the organization, the chief audit executive should discuss the matter with senior management. If the decision regarding residual risk is not resolved, the chief audit executive and senior management should report the matter to the board for resolution.

GLOSSARY

Add Value
Value is provided by improving opportunities to achieve organizational objectives, identifying operational improvement, and/or reducing risk exposure through both assurance and consulting services.

Adequate Control
Present if management has planned and organized (designed) in a manner that provides reasonable assurance that the organization's risks have been managed effectively and that the organization's goals and objectives will be achieved efficiently and economically.

Assurance Services
An objective examination of evidence for the purpose of providing an independent assessment on risk management, control, or governance processes for the organization. Examples may include financial, performance, compliance, system security, and due diligence engagements.

Board
A board is an organization's governing body, such as a board of directors, supervisory board, head of an agency or legislative body, board of governors or trustees of a nonprofit organization, or any other designated body of the organization, including the audit committee, to whom the chief audit executive may functionally report.

Charter
The charter of the internal audit activity is a formal written document that defines the activity's purpose, authority, and responsibility. The charter should (a) establish the internal audit activity's position within the organization; (b) authorize access to records, personnel, and physical properties relevant to the performance of engagements; and (c) define the scope of internal audit activities.

Chief Audit Executive

Top position within the organization responsible for internal audit activities. Normally, this would be the internal audit director. In the case where internal audit activities are obtained from outside service providers, the chief audit executive is the person responsible for overseeing the service contract and the overall quality assurance of these activities, reporting to senior management and the board regarding internal audit activities, and follow-up of engagement results. The term also includes such titles as general auditor, chief internal auditor, and inspector general.

Code of Ethics

The Code of Ethics of The Institute of Internal Auditors (IIA) are Principles relevant to the profession and practice of internal auditing, and Rules of Conduct that describe behavior expected of internal auditors. The Code of Ethics applies to both parties and entities that provide internal audit services. The purpose of the Code of Ethics is to promote an ethical culture in the global profession of internal auditing.

Compliance

Conformity and adherence to policies, plans, procedures, laws, regulations, contracts, or other requirements.

Conflict of Interest

Any relationship that is or appears to be not in the best interest of the organization. A conflict of interest would prejudice an individual's ability to perform his or her duties and responsibilities objectively.

Consulting Services

Advisory and related client service activities, the nature and scope of which are agreed with the client and which are intended to add value and improve an organization's governance, risk management, and control processes without the internal auditor assuming management responsibility. Examples include counsel, advice, facilitation, and training.

Control

Any action taken by management, the board, and other parties to manage risk and increase the likelihood that established objectives and goals will be achieved. Management plans, organizes, and directs the performance of sufficient actions to provide reasonable assurance that objectives and goals will be achieved.

Control Environment

The attitude and actions of the board and management regarding the significance of control within the organization. The control environment provides the discipline and structure for the achievement of the primary objectives of the system of internal control. The control environment includes the following elements:
- Integrity and ethical values.
- Management's philosophy and operating style.
- Organizational structure.
- Assignment of authority and responsibility.
- Human resource policies and practices.
- Competence of personnel.

Control Processes

The policies, procedures, and activities that are part of a control framework, designed to ensure that risks are contained within the risk tolerances established by the risk management process.

Engagement

A specific internal audit assignment, task, or review activity, such as an internal audit, control self-assessment review, fraud examination, or consultancy. An engagement may include multiple tasks or activities designed to accomplish a specific set of related objectives.

Engagement Objectives
Broad statements developed by internal auditors that define intended engagement accomplishments.

Engagement Work Program
A document that lists the procedures to be followed during an engagement, designed to achieve the engagement plan.

External Service Provider
A person or firm, outside of the organization, who has special knowledge, skill, and experience in a particular discipline.

Fraud
Any illegal acts characterized by deceit, concealment, or violation of trust. These acts are not dependent upon the application of threat of violence or of physical force. Frauds are perpetrated by parties and organizations to obtain money, property, or services; to avoid payment or loss of services; or to secure personal or business advantage.

Governance
The combination of processes and structures implemented by the board in order to inform, direct, manage, and monitor the activities of the organization toward the achievement of its objectives.

Impairments
Impairments to individual objectivity and organizational independence may include personal conflicts of interest, scope limitations, restrictions on access to records, personnel, and properties, and resource limitations (funding).

Independence
The freedom from conditions that threaten objectivity or the appearance of objectivity. Such threats to objectivity must be managed at the individual auditor, engagement, functional, and organizational levels.

Internal Audit Activity

A department, division, team of consultants, or other practitioner(s) that provides independent, objective assurance and consulting services designed to add value and improve an organization's operations. The internal audit activity helps an organization accomplish its objectives by bringing a systematic, disciplined approach to evaluate and improve the effectiveness of risk management, control, and governance processes.

Objectivity

An unbiased mental attitude that allows internal auditors to perform engagements in such a manner that they have an honest belief in their work product and that no significant quality compromises are made. Objectivity requires internal auditors not to subordinate their judgment on audit matters to that of others.

Residual Risk

The risk remaining after management takes action to reduce the impact and likelihood of an adverse event, including control activities in responding to a risk.

Risk

The possibility of an event occurring that will have an impact on the achievement of objectives. Risk is measured in terms of impact and likelihood.

Risk Management

A process to identify, assess, manage, and control potential events or situations to provide reasonable assurance regarding the achievement of the organization's objectives.

Should

The use of the word "should" in the *Standards* represents a mandatory obligation.

Standard
A professional pronouncement promulgated by the Internal Auditing Standards Board that delineates the requirements for performing a broad range of internal audit activities, and for evaluating internal audit performance.

PRACTICE
ADVISORIES

Practice Advisory 1000-1:
Internal Audit Charter

Interpretation of *Standard 1000* from the *International Standards for the Professional Practice of Internal Auditing*

> *Related Standard*
> **1000 – Purpose, Authority, and Responsibility**
> The purpose, authority, and responsibility of the internal audit activity should be formally defined in a charter, consistent with the *Standards*, and approved by the board.

Nature of this Practice Advisory: Internal auditors should consider the following suggestions when adopting an internal audit charter. This guidance is not intended to represent all the considerations that may be necessary when adopting a charter, but simply a recommended set of items that should be addressed.

1. The purpose, authority, and responsibility of the internal audit activity should be defined in a charter. The chief audit executive (CAE) should seek approval of the charter by senior management as well as acceptance by the board. The approval of the charter should be documented in the governing body minutes. The charter should (a) establish the internal audit activity's position within the organization; (b) authorize access to records, personnel, and physical properties relevant to the performance of engagements; and (c) define the scope of internal audit activities.

2. The internal audit activity's charter should be in writing. A written statement provides formal communication for review and approval by management and for acceptance by the board. It also facilitates a periodic assessment of the adequacy of the internal audit activity's purpose, authority, and responsibility. Providing a formal, written document containing the charter of the internal audit activity is critical in managing the auditing function within the organization. The purpose, authority, and responsibility should be defined and communicated to establish the role of the internal audit activity and to provide a basis for management and the board to use in evaluating the operations of the function. If a question should arise, the charter also provides a formal, written agreement with management and the board about the role and responsibilities of the internal audit activity within the organization.

3. The CAE should periodically assess whether the purpose, authority, and responsibility, as defined in the charter, continue to be adequate to enable the internal audit activity to accomplish its objectives. The result of this periodic assessment should be communicated to senior management and the board.

Practice Advisory 1000.C1-1: Principles Guiding the Performance of Consulting Activities of Internal Auditors

Interpretation of *Standard 1000.C1* from the *International Standards for the Professional Practice of Internal Auditing*

> ***Related Standard***
> **1000.C1** – The nature of consulting services should be defined in the audit charter.

Nature of this Practice Advisory: The definition of internal auditing states: "Internal auditing is an independent, objective assurance and consulting activity designed to add value and improve an organization's operations. It helps an organization accomplish its objectives by bringing a systematic, disciplined approach to evaluate and improve the effectiveness of risk management, control, and governance processes." Internal auditors are reminded that the Attribute and Performance Standards relate to internal auditors performing both assurance and consulting engagements.

This advisory focuses on broad parameters to be considered in all consulting engagements. Consulting may range from formal engagements, defined by written agreements, to advisory activities, such as participating in standing or temporary management committees or project teams. Internal auditors are expected to use professional judgment to determine the extent to which the guidance provided in this advisory should be applied in each given situation. Special consulting engagements, such as participation in a merger or acquisition project, or in emergency engagements, such as disaster recovery activities, may require departure from normal or established procedures for conducting consulting engagements.

Internal auditors should consider the following guiding principles when performing consulting engagements. This guidance is not intended to represent all the considerations that may be necessary in performing a consulting engagement and internal auditors should take extra precautions to determine that management and the board understand and agree with the concept, operating guidelines, and communications required for performing consulting services.

1. **Value Proposition** — The value proposition of the internal audit activity is realized within every organization that employs internal auditors in a manner that suits the culture and resources of that organization. That value proposition is captured in the definition of internal auditing and includes assurance and consulting activities designed to add value to the organization by bringing a systematic, disciplined approach to the areas of governance, risk, and control.

2. **Consistency with Internal Audit Definition** — A disciplined, systematic evaluation methodology is incorporated in each internal audit activity. The list of services can generally be incorporated into the broad categories of assurance and consulting. However, the services may also include evolving forms of value-adding services that are consistent with the broad definition of internal auditing.

3. **Audit Activities Beyond Assurance and Consulting** — There are multiple internal auditing services. Assurance and consulting are not mutually exclusive and do not preclude other

auditing services such as investigations and non-auditing roles. Many audit services will have both an assurance and consultative (advising) role.

4. **Interrelationship Between Assurance and Consulting** — Internal audit consulting enriches value-adding internal auditing. While consulting is often the direct result of assurance services, it should also be recognized that assurance could also be generated from consulting engagements.

5. **Empower Consulting Through the Internal Audit Charter** — Internal auditors have traditionally performed many types of consulting services ranging from the analysis of controls built into developing systems, analysis of security products, serving on task forces to analyze operations and make recommendations, and so forth. The board (or audit committee) should empower the internal audit activity to perform additional services where they do not represent a conflict of interest or detract from its obligations to the committee. That empowerment should be reflected in the internal audit charter.

6. **Objectivity** — Consulting services may enhance the auditor's understanding of business processes or issues related to an assurance engagement and do not necessarily impair the auditor's or the internal audit activity's objectivity. Internal auditing is not a management decision-making function. Decisions to adopt or implement recommendations made as a result of an internal audit advisory service should be made by management. Therefore internal audit objectivity should not be impaired by the decisions made by management.

7. **Internal Audit Foundation for Consulting Services** — Much of consulting is a natural extension of assurance and investigative services and may represent informal or formal advice, analysis, or assessments. The internal audit activity is uniquely positioned

to perform this type of consulting work based on (a) its adherence to the highest standards of objectivity; and (b) its breadth of knowledge about organizational processes, risks, and strategies.

8. **Communication of Fundamental Information** — A primary internal audit value is to provide assurance to senior management and audit committee directors. Consulting engagements cannot be rendered in a manner that masks information that in the chief audit executive's (CAE) judgment should be presented to senior executives and board members. All consulting is to be understood in that context.

9. **Principles of Consulting Understood by the Organization** — Organizations must have ground rules for the performance of consulting services that are understood by all members of an organization and these rules should be codified in the audit charter approved by the audit committee and promulgated in the organization.

10. **Formal Consulting Engagements** — Management often engages outside consultants for formal consulting engagements that last a significant period of time. However, an organization may find that the internal audit activity is uniquely qualified for some formal consulting tasks. If an internal audit activity undertakes to perform a formal consulting engagement, the internal audit group should bring a systematic, disciplined approach to the conduct of the engagement.

11. **CAE Responsibilities** — Consulting services permit the CAE to enter into dialog with management to address specific managerial issues. In this dialog, the breadth of the engagement and time frames are made responsive to management needs. However, the CAE retains the prerogative of setting the audit techniques and the right of reporting to senior executives and

audit committee members when the nature and materiality of results pose significant risks to the organization.

12. **Criteria for Resolving Conflicts or Evolving Issues** — An internal auditor is first and foremost an internal auditor. Thus, in the performance of all services the internal auditor is guided by The IIA's Code of Ethics and the Attribute and Performance Standards of the *International Standards for the Professional Practice of Internal Auditing (Standards)*. Any unforeseen conflicts or activities should be resolved consistent with the Code of Ethics and *Standards*.

Practice Advisory 1000.C1-2:
Additional Considerations for
Formal Consulting Engagements

**Interpretation of *Standard 1000.C1* (and other
related Consulting Implementation Standards) from the
*International Standards for the
Professional Practice of Internal Auditing***

Related Standard
1000.C1 – The nature of consulting services should be defined
in the audit charter.

Special note regarding this Practice Advisory and related
Standards. This Practice Advisory includes guidance related to
multiple *Consulting Implementation Standards*. In addition to
Standard 1000.C1, the guidance also covers *Standards
1130.C1* and *C2; 1210.C1; 1220.C1; 2010.C1; 2110.C1* and
C2; 2120.C1 and *C2; 2130.C1; 2201.C1; 2210.C1; 2220.C1;
2240.C1; 2330.C1; 2410.C1; 2440.C1* and *C2;* and *2500.C1.*
References to those *Standards* are shown parenthetically in the
headings of this Practice Advisory.

Nature of this Practice Advisory: *This Practice Advisory is similar
in subject matter to Practice Advisory 1000.C1-1, which
discusses the Principles Guiding the Performance of Consulting
Services, and both advisories are useful to internal auditors in
performing consulting activities. The definition of internal
auditing states: "Internal auditing is an independent, objective
assurance and **consulting** activity designed to add value and
improve an organization's operations. It helps an organization*

accomplish its objectives by bringing a systematic, disciplined approach to evaluate and improve the effectiveness of risk management, control, and governance processes." Internal auditors are reminded that the Attribute and Performance Standards relate to internal auditors performing both assurance and consulting engagements.

This Practice Advisory focuses on broad parameters to be considered in formal consulting engagements. Consulting may range from formal engagements, defined by written agreements, to advisory activities, such as participating in standing or temporary management committees or project teams. Internal auditors are expected to use professional judgment to determine the extent to which the guidance provided in this advisory should be applied in each given situation. Special consulting engagements, such as participation in a merger or acquisition project and in an emergency engagement (for example, a review of disaster recovery activities), may require departure from normal or established procedures for conducting consulting engagements.

Internal auditors should consider the following suggestions when performing formal consulting engagements. This guidance is not intended to represent all the considerations that may be necessary in performing a consulting engagement and internal auditors should take extra precautions to determine that management and the board understand and agree with the concept, operating guidelines, and communications required for performing formal consulting services.

Definition of Consulting Services

1. The Glossary in the *International Standards for the Professional Practice of Internal Auditing (Standards)* defines "consulting services" as follows: "Advisory and related client service activities, the nature and scope of which are agreed with the client and which are intended to add value and improve an organization's governance, risk management, and control processes without the internal auditor assuming management responsibility. Examples include counsel, advice, facilitation, and training."

2. The chief audit executive (CAE) should determine the methodology to use for classifying engagements within the organization. In some circumstances, it may be appropriate to conduct a "blended" engagement that incorporates elements of both consulting and assurance activities into one consolidated approach. In other cases, it may be appropriate to distinguish between the assurance and consulting components of the engagement.

3. Internal auditors may conduct consulting services as part of their normal or routine activities as well as in response to requests by management. Each organization should consider the type of consulting activities to be offered and determine if specific policies or procedures should be developed for each type of activity. Possible categories could include:
    *   Formal consulting engagements — planned and subject to written agreement.
    *   Informal consulting engagements — routine activities, such as participation on standing committees, limited-life projects, ad hoc meetings, and routine information exchange.
    *   Special consulting engagements — participation on a merger and acquisition team or system conversion team.

- Emergency consulting engagements — participation on a team established for recovery or maintenance of operations after a disaster or other extraordinary business event or a team assembled to supply temporary help to meet a special request or unusual deadline.

4. Auditors generally should not agree to conduct a consulting engagement simply to circumvent, or to allow others to circumvent, requirements that would normally apply to an assurance engagement if the service in question is more appropriately conducted as an assurance engagement. This does not preclude adjusting methodologies where services once conducted as assurance engagements are deemed more suitable to being performed as a consulting engagement.

Independence and Objectivity in Consulting Engagements (*Standard 1130.C1*)

5. Internal auditors are sometimes requested to provide consulting services relating to operations for which they had previous responsibilities or had conducted assurance services. Prior to offering consulting services, the CAE should confirm that the board understands and approves the concept of providing consulting services. Once approved, the internal audit charter should be amended to include authority and responsibilities for consulting activities, and the internal audit activity should develop appropriate policies and procedures for conducting such engagements.

6. Internal auditors should maintain their objectivity when drawing conclusions and offering advice to management. If impairments to independence or objectivity exist prior to commencement of the consulting engagement, or subsequently develop during the engagement, disclosure should be made immediately to management.

7. Independence and objectivity may be impaired if assurance services are provided within one year after a formal consulting engagement. Steps can be taken to minimize the effects of impairment by assigning different auditors to perform each of the services, establishing independent management and supervision, defining separate accountability for the results of the projects, and disclosing the presumed impairment. Management should be responsible for accepting and implementing recommendations.

8. Care should be taken, particularly involving consulting engagements that are ongoing or continuous in nature, so that internal auditors do not inappropriately or unintentionally assume management responsibilities that were not intended in the original objectives and scope of the engagement.

Due Professional Care in Consulting Engagements
(Standards 1210.C1, 1220.C1, 2130.C1, and 2201.C1)

9. The internal auditor should exercise due professional care in conducting a formal consulting engagement by understanding the following:
    *   Needs of management officials, including the nature, timing, and communication of engagement results.
    *   Possible motivations and reasons of those requesting the service.
    *   Extent of work needed to achieve the engagement's objectives.
    *   Skills and resources needed to conduct the engagement.
    *   Effect on the scope of the audit plan previously approved by the audit committee.
    *   Potential impact on future audit assignments and engagements.
    *   Potential organizational benefits to be derived from the engagement.

10. In addition to the independence and objectivity evaluation and due professional care considerations described above, the internal auditor should:

- Conduct appropriate meetings and gather necessary information to assess the nature and extent of the service to be provided.
- Confirm that those receiving the service understand and agree with the relevant guidance contained in the internal audit charter, internal audit activity's policies and procedures, and other related guidance governing the conduct of consulting engagements. The internal auditor should decline to perform consulting engagements that are prohibited by the terms of the internal audit charter, conflict with the policies and procedures of the internal audit activity, or do not add value and promote the best interests of the organization.
- Evaluate the consulting engagement for compatibility with the internal audit activity's overall plan of engagements. The internal audit activity's risk-based plan of engagements may incorporate and rely on consulting engagements, to the extent deemed appropriate, to provide necessary audit coverage to the organization.
- Document general terms, understandings, deliverables, and other key factors of the formal consulting engagement in a written agreement or plan. It is essential that both the internal auditor and those receiving the consulting engagement understand and agree with the reporting and communication requirements.

Scope of Work in Consulting Engagements
(Standards 2010.C1, 2110.C1 and C2, 2120.C1 and C2, 2201.C1, 2210.C1, 2220.C1, 2240.C1, and 2440.C2)

11. As observed above, internal auditors should reach an understanding about the objectives and scope of the consulting engagement with those receiving the service. Any reservations

about the value, benefit, or possible negative implications of the consulting engagement should be communicated to those receiving the service. Internal auditors should design the scope of work to ensure that professionalism, integrity, credibility, and reputation of the internal audit activity will be maintained.

12. In planning formal consulting engagements, internal auditors should design objectives to meet the appropriate needs of management officials receiving these services. In the case of special requests by management, internal auditors may consider the following actions if they believe that the objectives that should be pursued go beyond those requested by management:
    • Persuade management to include the additional objectives in the consulting engagement; or
    • Document the fact that the objectives were not pursued and disclose that observation in the final communication of consulting engagement results; and
    • Include the objectives in a separate and subsequent assurance engagement.

13. Work programs for formal consulting engagements should document the objectives and scope of the engagement as well as the methodology to be used in satisfying the objectives. The form and content of the program may vary depending on the nature of the engagement. In establishing the scope of the engagement, internal auditors may expand or limit the scope to satisfy management's request. However, the internal auditor should be satisfied that the projected scope of work will be adequate to meet the objectives of the engagement. The objectives, scope, and terms of the engagement should be periodically reassessed and adjusted during the course of the work.

14. Internal auditors should be observant of the effectiveness of risk management and control processes during formal consulting

engagements. Substantial risk exposures or material control weaknesses should be brought to the attention of management. In some situations the auditor's concerns should also be communicated to executive management, the audit committee, and/or the board of directors. Auditors should use professional judgment (a) to determine the significance of exposures or weaknesses and the actions taken or contemplated to mitigate or correct these exposures or weaknesses and (b) to ascertain the expectations of executive management, the audit committee, and board in having these matters reported.

Communicating the Results of Consulting Engagements (Standards 2410.C1 and 2440.C1)

15. Communication of the progress and results of consulting engagements will vary in form and content depending upon the nature of the engagement and the needs of the client. Reporting requirements are generally determined by those requesting the consulting service and should meet the objectives as determined and agreed to with management. However, the format for communicating the results of the consulting engagement should clearly describe the nature of the engagement and any limitations, restrictions, or other factors about which users of the information should be made aware.

16. In some circumstances, the internal auditor may conclude that the results should be communicated beyond those who received or requested the service. In such cases, the internal auditor should expand the reporting so that results are communicated to the appropriate parties. When expanding the reporting to other parties, the auditor should conduct the following steps until satisfied with the resolution of the matter:
    • First, determine what direction is provided in the agreement concerning the consulting engagement and related communications.

- Second, attempt to convince those receiving or requesting the service to expand voluntarily the communication to the appropriate parties.
- Third, determine what guidance is provided in the internal audit charter or audit activity's policies and procedures concerning consulting communications.
- Fourth, determine what guidance is provided in the organization's code of conduct, code of ethics, and other relative policies, administrative directives, or procedures.
- Fifth, determine what guidance is provided by The IIA's *Standards* and Code of Ethics, other standards or codes applicable to the auditor, and any legal or regulatory requirements that relate to the matter under consideration.

17. Internal auditors should disclose to management, the audit committee, board, or other governing body of the organization the nature, extent, and overall results of formal consulting engagements along with other reports of internal auditing activities. Internal auditors should keep executive management and the audit committee informed about how audit resources are being deployed. Neither detail reports of these consulting engagements nor the specific results and recommendations are required to be communicated. But, an appropriate description of these types of engagements and their significant recommendations should be communicated and is essential in satisfying the internal auditor's responsibility in complying with *Standard 2060, Reporting to the Board and Senior Management.*

Documentation Requirements for Consulting Engagements *(Standard 2330.C1)*

18. Internal auditors should document the work performed to achieve the objectives of a formal consulting engagement and support its results. However, documentation requirements applicable to

assurance engagements do not necessarily apply to consulting engagements.

19. Auditors are encouraged to adopt appropriate record retention policies and address related issues, such as ownership of consulting engagement records, in order to protect the organization adequately and to avoid potential misunderstandings involving requests for these records. Situations involving legal proceedings, regulatory requirements, tax issues, and accounting matters may call for special handling of certain consulting engagement records.

Monitoring of Consulting Engagements
(Standard 2500.C1)

20. The internal audit activity should monitor the results of consulting engagements to the extent agreed upon with the client. Varying types of monitoring may be appropriate for differing types of consulting engagements. The monitoring effort may depend on factors such as management's explicit interest in the engagement or the internal auditor's assessment of the project's risks or value to the organization.

Practice Advisory 1100-1: Independence and Objectivity

Interpretation of *Standard 1100* from the *International Standards for the Professional Practice of Internal Auditing*

> *Related Standard*
> **1100 – Independence and Objectivity**
> The internal audit activity should be independent, and internal auditors should be objective in performing their work.

Nature of this Practice Advisory: Internal auditors should consider the following suggestions when evaluating independence and objectivity. This guidance is not intended to represent all the considerations that may be necessary when conducting such an evaluation, but simply a recommended set of items that should be addressed.

1. Internal auditors are independent when they can carry out their work freely and objectively. Independence permits internal auditors to render the impartial and unbiased judgments essential to the proper conduct of engagements. It is achieved through organizational status and objectivity.

Practice Advisory 1110-1: Organizational Independence

Interpretation of *Standard 1110* from the *International Standards for the Professional Practice of Internal Auditing*

Related Standard
1110 – Organizational Independence
The chief audit executive should report to a level within the organization that allows the internal audit activity to accomplish its responsibilities.

Nature of this Practice Advisory: *Internal auditors should consider the following suggestions when evaluating organizational independence. This guidance is not intended to represent all the considerations that may be necessary during such an evaluation, but simply a recommended set of items that should be addressed.*

1. Internal auditors should have the support of senior management and the board so that they can gain the cooperation of engagement clients and perform their work free from interference.

2. The chief audit executive (CAE) should be responsible to an individual in the organization with sufficient authority to promote independence and to ensure broad audit coverage, adequate consideration of engagement communications, and appropriate action on engagement recommendations.

3. Ideally, the CAE should report functionally to the board and administratively to the chief executive officer of the organization.

4. The CAE should have direct communication with the board. Regular communication with the board helps assure independence and provides a means for the board and the CAE to keep each other informed on matters of mutual interest.

5. Direct communication occurs when the CAE regularly attends and participates in meetings of the board, which relate to its oversight responsibilities for auditing, financial reporting, organizational governance, and control. The CAE's attendance and participation at these meetings provide an opportunity to be appraised of strategic business and operational developments, and to raise high-level risk, systems, procedures, or control type issues at an early stage. The opportunity is also provided to exchange information concerning the plans and activities of the internal auditing activity. The CAE should meet privately with the board, at least annually.

6. Independence is enhanced when the board concurs in the appointment or removal of the CAE.

Practice Advisory 1110-2:
Chief Audit Executive (CAE)
Reporting Lines

**Interpretation of *Standard 1110* from the
*International Standards for the
Professional Practice of Internal Auditing***

Related Standard
1110 – Organizational Independence
The chief audit executive should report to a level within the
organization that allows the internal audit activity to accomplish
its responsibilities.

*Nature of this Practice Advisory: Internal auditors should
consider the following guidance when establishing or evaluating
the reporting lines and relationships with organizational officials
to whom the CAE reports. This guidance is not intended to
represent all the considerations that may be necessary during
such an evaluation, but simply a recommended set of items that
should be considered.*

1. The IIA's *International Standards for the Professional
    Practice of Internal Auditing (Standards)* require that the chief
    audit executive (CAE) report to a level within the organization
    that allows the internal audit activity to fulfill its
    responsibilities. The IIA believes strongly that to achieve
    necessary independence, the CAE should report functionally to
    the audit committee or its equivalent. For administrative purposes,
    in most circumstances, the CAE should report directly to the

chief executive officer of the organization. The following descriptions of what The IIA considers "functional reporting" and "administrative reporting" are provided to help focus the discussion in this Practice Advisory.

- Functional Reporting — The functional reporting line for the internal audit function is the ultimate source of its independence and authority. As such, The IIA recommends that the CAE report functionally to the audit committee, board of directors, or other appropriate governing authority. In this context, report functionally means that the governing authority would:
  - Approve the overall charter of the internal audit function.
  - Approve the internal audit risk assessment and related audit plan.
  - Receive communications from the CAE on the results of the internal audit activities or other matters that the CAE determines are necessary, including private meetings with the CAE without management present.
  - Approve all decisions regarding the appointment or removal of the CAE.
  - Approve the annual compensation and salary adjustment of the CAE.
  - Make appropriate inquiries of management and the CAE to determine whether there are scope or budgetary limitations that impede the ability of the internal audit function to execute its responsibilities.
- Administrative Reporting — Administrative reporting is the reporting relationship within the organization's management structure that facilitates the day-to-day operations of the internal audit function. Administrative reporting typically includes:
  - Budgeting and management accounting.
  - Human resource administration, including personnel evaluations and compensation.

- Internal communications and information flows.
- Administration of the organization's internal policies and procedures.

2. This advisory focuses on considerations in establishing or evaluating CAE reporting lines. Appropriate reporting lines are critical to achieve the independence, objectivity, and organizational stature for an internal audit function necessary to effectively fulfill its obligations. CAE reporting lines are also critical to ensuring the appropriate flow of information and access to key executives and managers that are the foundations of risk assessment and reporting of results of audit activities. Conversely, any reporting relationship that impedes the independence and effective operations of the internal audit function should be viewed by the CAE as a serious scope limitation, which should be brought to the attention of the audit committee or its equivalent.

3. This advisory also recognizes that CAE reporting lines are impacted by the nature of the organization (public or private as well as relative size); common practices of each country; growing complexity of organizations (joint ventures, multinational corporations with subsidiaries); and the trend toward internal audit groups providing value-added services with increased collaboration on priorities and scope with their clients. Accordingly, while The IIA believes that there is an ideal reporting structure with functional reporting to the audit committee and administrative reporting to the CEO, other relationships can be effective if there are clear distinctions between the functional and administrative reporting lines and appropriate activities are in each line to ensure that the independence and scope of activities are maintained. Internal auditors are expected to use professional judgment to determine the extent to which the guidance provided in this advisory should be applied in each given situation.

4. The *Standards* stress the importance of the CAE reporting to an individual with sufficient authority to promote independence and to ensure broad audit coverage. The *Standards* are purposely somewhat generic about reporting relationships, however, because they are designed to be applicable at all organizations regardless of size or any other factors. Factors that make "one size fits all" unattainable include organization size and type of organization (private, governmental, corporate). Accordingly, the CAE should consider the following attributes in evaluating the appropriateness of the administrative reporting line.

    *   Does the individual have sufficient authority and stature to ensure the effectiveness of the function?
    *   Does the individual have an appropriate control and governance mind-set to assist the CAE in their role?
    *   Does the individual have the time and interest to actively support the CAE on audit issues?
    *   Does the individual understand the functional reporting relationship and support it?

5. The CAE should also ensure that appropriate independence is maintained if the individual responsible for the administrative reporting line is also responsible for other activities in the organization, which are subject to internal audit. For example, some CAEs report administratively to the chief financial officer, who is also responsible for the organization's accounting functions. The internal audit function should be free to audit and report on any activity that also reports to its administrative head if it deems that coverage appropriate for its audit plan. Any limitation in scope or reporting of results of these activities should be brought to the attention of the audit committee.

6. Under the recent move to a stricter legislative and regulatory climate regarding financial reporting around the globe, the CAE's reporting lines should be appropriate to enable the internal audit activity to meet any increased needs of the audit committee or

other significant stakeholders. Increasingly, the CAE is being asked to take a more significant role in the organization's governance and risk management activities. The reporting lines of the CAE should facilitate the ability of the internal audit activity to meet these expectations.

7. Regardless of which reporting relationship the organization chooses, several key actions can help assure that the reporting lines support and enable the effectiveness and independence of the internal auditing activity.
    - Functional Reporting:
        - The functional reporting line should go directly to the audit committee or its equivalent to ensure the appropriate level of independence and communication.
        - The CAE should meet privately with the audit committee or its equivalent, without management present, to reinforce the independence and nature of this reporting relationship.
        - The audit committee should have the final authority to review and approve the annual audit plan and all major changes to the plan.
        - At all times, the CAE should have open and direct access to the chair of the audit committee and its members; or the chair of the board or full board if appropriate.
        - At least once a year, the audit committee should review the performance of the CAE and approve the annual compensation and salary adjustment.
        - The charter for the internal audit function should clearly articulate both the functional and administrative reporting lines for the function as well as the principle activities directed up each line.
    - Administrative Reporting:
        - The administrative reporting line of the CAE should be to the CEO or another executive with sufficient authority to afford it appropriate support to accomplish its day-

to-day activities. This support should include positioning the function and the CAE in the organization's structure in a manner that affords appropriate stature for the function within the organization. Reporting too low in an organization can negatively impact the stature and effectiveness of the internal audit function.

- The administrative reporting line should not have ultimate authority over the scope or reporting of results of the internal audit activity.
- The administrative reporting line should facilitate open and direct communications with executive and line management. The CAE should be able to communicate directly with any level of management, including the CEO.
- The administrative reporting line should enable adequate communications and information flow such that the CAE and the internal audit function have an adequate and timely flow of information concerning the activities, plans, and business initiatives of the organization.
- Budgetary controls and considerations imposed by the administrative reporting line should not impede the ability of the internal audit function to accomplish its mission.

8. CAEs should also consider their relationships with other control and monitoring functions (risk management, compliance, security, legal, ethics, environmental, external audit) and facilitate the reporting of material risk and control issues to the audit committee.

Practice Advisory 1110.A1-1:
Disclosing Reasons for
Information Requests

**Interpretation of *Standard 1110.A1* from the
*International Standards for the
Professional Practice of Internal Auditing***

Related Standard
1110.A1 – The internal audit activity should be free from interference in determining the scope of internal auditing, performing work, and communicating results.

Nature of this Practice Advisory: *Internal auditors should consider the following suggestions when requested to disclose reasons for information requests. This guidance is not intended to represent all the considerations that may be necessary, but simply a recommended set of items that should be addressed.*

1. At times, an internal auditor may be asked by the engagement client or other parties to explain why a document that has been requested is relevant to an engagement. Disclosure or nondisclosure during the engagement of the reasons why documents are needed should be determined based on the circumstances. Significant irregularities may dictate a less open environment than would normally be conducive to a cooperative engagement. However, that is a judgment that should be made by the chief audit executive in light of the specific circumstances.

Practice Advisory 1120-1: Individual Objectivity

Interpretation of *Standard 1120* from the *International Standards for the Professional Practice of Internal Auditing*

> ***Related Standard***
> **1120 – Individual Objectivity**
> Internal auditors should have an impartial, unbiased attitude and avoid conflicts of interest.

Nature of this Practice Advisory: *Internal auditors should consider the following suggestions when evaluating individual objectivity. This guidance is not intended to represent all the considerations that may be necessary during such an evaluation, but simply a recommended set of items that should be addressed.*

1. Objectivity is an independent mental attitude which internal auditors should maintain in performing engagements. Internal auditors are not to subordinate their judgment on audit matters to that of others.

2. Objectivity requires internal auditors to perform engagements in such a manner that they have an honest belief in their work product and that no significant quality compromises are made. Internal auditors are not to be placed in situations in which they feel unable to make objective professional judgments.

3. Staff assignments should be made so that potential and actual conflicts of interest and bias are avoided. The chief audit executive should periodically obtain from the internal auditing staff information concerning potential conflicts of interest and bias. Staff assignments of internal auditors should be rotated periodically whenever it is practicable to do so.

4. The results of internal audit work should be reviewed before the related engagement communications are released to provide reasonable assurance that the work was performed objectively.

5. It is unethical for an internal auditor to accept a fee, gift, or entertainment from an employee, client, customer, supplier, or business associate. Accepting a fee, gift, or entertainment may create an appearance that the auditor's objectivity has been impaired. The appearance that objectivity has been impaired may apply to current and future engagements conducted by the auditor. The status of engagements should not be considered as justification for receiving fees, gifts, or entertainment. The receipt of promotional items (such as pens, calendars, or samples) that are available to employees and the general public which have minimal value should not hinder internal auditors' professional judgments. Internal auditors should report the offer of all material fees or gifts immediately to their supervisors.

6. The internal audit activity should adopt a policy that addresses its commitment to conduct activities so as to avoid conflicts of interest and to disclose any activities that could result in a possible conflict of interest.

Practice Advisory 1130-1:
Impairments to
Independence or Objectivity

**Interpretation of *Standard 1130* from the
*International Standards for the
Professional Practice of Internal Auditing***

Related Standard
1130 – Impairments to Independence or Objectivity
If independence or objectivity is impaired in fact or appearance,
the details of the impairment should be disclosed to appropriate
parties. The nature of the disclosure will depend upon the
impairment.

Nature of this Practice Advisory: *Internal auditors should
consider the following suggestions when evaluating impairments
to independence or objectivity. This guidance is not intended
to represent all the considerations that may be necessary during
such an evaluation, but simply a recommended set of items that
should be addressed.*

1. Internal auditors should report to the chief audit executive (CAE)
    any situations in which a conflict of interest or bias is present or
    may reasonably be inferred. The CAE should then reassign
    such auditors.

2. A scope limitation is a restriction placed upon the internal audit
    activity that precludes the audit activity from accomplishing its

objectives and plans. Among other things, a scope limitation may restrict the:
- Scope defined in the charter.
- Internal audit activity's access to records, personnel, and physical properties relevant to the performance of engagements.
- Approved engagement work schedule.
- Performance of necessary engagement procedures.
- Approved staffing plan and financial budget.

3. A scope limitation along with its potential effect should be communicated, preferably in writing, to the board.

4. The CAE should consider whether it is appropriate to inform the board regarding scope limitations that were previously communicated to and accepted by the board. This may be necessary particularly when there have been organization, board, senior management, or other changes.

Practice Advisory 1130.A1-1: Assessing Operations for Which Internal Auditors Were Previously Responsible

Interpretation of *Standard 1130.A1* from the *International Standards for the Professional Practice of Internal Auditing*

> *Related Standard*
> **1130.A1** – Internal auditors should refrain from assessing specific operations for which they were previously responsible. Objectivity is presumed to be impaired if an auditor provides assurance services for an activity for which the auditor had responsibility within the previous year.

Nature of this Practice Advisory: Internal auditors should consider the following suggestions when faced with a situation where the auditor has been assigned to assess an operation for which they were previously responsible. This guidance is not intended to represent all the considerations that may be necessary during such an evaluation, but simply a recommended set of items that should be addressed.

1. Internal auditors should not assume operating responsibilities. If senior management directs internal auditors to perform non-audit work, it should be understood that they are not functioning as internal auditors. Moreover, objectivity is presumed to be impaired when internal auditors perform an assurance review of any activity for which they had authority or responsibility within the

past year. This impairment should be considered when communicating audit engagement results.

- If internal auditors are directed to perform non-audit duties that may impair objectivity, such as preparation of bank reconciliations, the chief audit executive should inform senior management and the board that this activity is not an assurance audit activity; and, therefore, audit-related conclusions should not be drawn.

- In addition, when operating responsibilities are assigned to the internal audit activity, special attention must be given to ensure objectivity when a subsequent assurance engagement in the related operating area is undertaken. Objectivity is presumed to be impaired when internal auditors audit any activity for which they had authority or responsibility within the past year. These facts should be clearly stated when communicating the results of an audit engagement relating to an area where an auditor had operating responsibilities.

2. At any point that assigned activities involve the assumption of operating authority, audit objectivity would be presumed to be impaired with respect to that activity.

3. Persons transferred to or temporarily engaged by the internal audit activity should not be assigned to audit those activities they previously performed until a reasonable period of time (at least one year) has elapsed. Such assignments are presumed to impair objectivity, and additional consideration should be exercised when supervising the engagement work and communicating engagement results.

4. The internal auditor's objectivity is not adversely affected when the auditor recommends standards of control for systems or reviews procedures before they are implemented. The auditor's

objectivity is considered to be impaired if the auditor designs, installs, drafts procedures for, or operates such systems.

5. The occasional performance of non-audit work by the internal auditor, with full disclosure in the reporting process, would not necessarily impair independence. However, it would require careful consideration by management and the internal auditor to avoid adversely affecting the internal auditor's objectivity.

Practice Advisory 1130.A1-2:
Internal Auditing's Responsibility
for Other (Non-audit) Functions

Interpretation of *Standard 1130.A1* **from the**
International Standards for the
Professional Practice of Internal Auditing

Related Standard
1130.A1 – Internal auditors should refrain from assessing specific operations for which they were previously responsible. Objectivity is presumed to be impaired if an auditor provides assurance services for an activity for which the auditor had responsibility within the previous year.

Nature of this Practice Advisory: The following guidance is offered to internal auditors faced with accepting responsibility for non-audit, operational functions or duties. Acceptance of such responsibilities can impair independence and objectivity and, if possible, should be avoided. This guidance is not intended to represent all the considerations that may be necessary in evaluating such responsibilities or assignments.

1. Some internal auditors have been assigned or accepted non-audit duties due to a variety of business reasons that make sense to management of the organization. Internal auditors are more frequently being asked to perform roles and responsibilities that may impair independence or objectivity. Given the increasing demand on organizations, both public and private, to develop more efficient and effective operations and to do so with fewer

resources, some internal audit activities are being directed by their organization's management to assume responsibility for operations that are subject to periodic internal auditing assessments.

2. When the internal audit activity or individual internal auditor is responsible for, or management is considering assigning, an operation that it might audit, the internal auditor's independence and objectivity may be impaired. The internal auditor should consider the following factors in assessing the impact on independence and objectivity:
    *   The requirements of The IIA's Code of Ethics and *International Standards for the Professional Practice of Internal Auditing (Standards)*;
    *   Expectations of stakeholders that may include the shareholders, board of directors, audit committee, management, legislative bodies, public entities, regulatory bodies, and public interest groups;
    *   Allowances and/or restrictions contained in the internal audit activity charter;
    *   Disclosures required by the *Standards*; and
    *   Subsequent audit coverage of the activities or responsibilities accepted by the internal auditor.

3. Internal auditors should consider the following factors to determine an appropriate course of action when presented with the opportunity of accepting responsibility for a non-audit function:
    A. The IIA's Code of Ethics and *Standards* require the internal audit activity to be independent, and internal auditors to be objective in performing their work.
        *   If possible, internal auditors should avoid accepting responsibility for non-audit functions or duties that are subject to periodic internal auditing assessments. If this is not possible, then;

- Impairment to independence and objectivity are required to be disclosed to appropriate parties, and the nature of the disclosure depends upon the impairment.
- Objectivity is presumed to be impaired if an auditor provides assurance services for an activity for which the auditor had responsibility within the previous year.
- If on occasion management directs internal auditors to perform non-audit work, it should be understood that they are not functioning as internal auditors.

B. Expectations of stakeholders, including regulatory or legal requirements, should be evaluated and assessed in relation to the potential impairment.

C. If the internal audit activity charter contains specific restrictions or limiting language regarding the assignment of non-audit functions to the internal auditor, then these restrictions should be disclosed and discussed with management. If management insists on such an assignment, the auditor should disclose and discuss this matter with the audit committee or appropriate governing body. If the charter is silent on this matter, the guidance noted in the points below should be considered. All the points noted below are subordinated to the language of the charter.

D. **Assessment** — The results of the assessment should be discussed with management, the audit committee, and/or other appropriate stakeholders. A determination should be made regarding a number of issues, some of which affect one another:
- The significance of the operational function to the organization (in terms of revenue, expenses, reputation, and influence) should be evaluated.
- The length or duration of the assignment and scope of responsibility should be evaluated.

- Adequacy of separation of duties should be evaluated.
- The potential impairment to objectivity or independence or the appearance of such impairment should be considered when reporting audit results.

E. **Audit of the Function and Disclosure** — Given that the internal audit activity has operational responsibilities and that operation is part of the audit plan, there are several avenues for the auditor to consider.

- The audit may be performed by a contracted, third-party entity, by external auditors, or by the internal audit function. In the first two situations, impairment of objectivity is minimized by the use of auditors outside the organization. In the latter case, objectivity would be impaired.
- Individual auditors with operational responsibility should not participate in the audit of the operation. If possible, auditors conducting the assessment should be supervised by, and report the results of the assessment to, those whose independence or objectivity is not impaired.
- Disclosure should be made regarding the operational responsibilities of the auditor for the function, the significance of the operation to the organization (in terms of revenue, expenses, or other pertinent information), and the relationship of those who audited the function to the auditor.
- Disclosure of the auditor's operational responsibilities should be made in the related audit report and in the auditor's standard communication to the audit committee or other governing body.

Practice Advisory 1200-1: Proficiency and Due Professional Care

Interpretation of *Standard 1200* from the *International Standards for the Professional Practice of Internal Auditing*

> ***Related Standard***
> **1200 – Proficiency and Due Professional Care**
> Engagements should be performed with proficiency and due professional care.

Nature of this Practice Advisory: *Internal auditors should consider the following suggestions when performing engagements. This guidance is not intended to represent all the considerations that may be necessary, but simply a recommended set of items that should be addressed.*

1. Professional proficiency is the responsibility of the chief audit executive (CAE) and each internal auditor. The CAE should ensure that persons assigned to each engagement collectively possess the necessary knowledge, skills, and other competencies to conduct the engagement properly.

2. Internal auditors should comply with professional standards of conduct. The IIA's Code of Ethics extends beyond the definition of internal auditing to include two essential components:

- Principles that are relevant to the profession and practice of internal auditing: integrity, objectivity, confidentiality, and competency; and
- Rules of conduct that describe behavior norms expected of internal auditors. These rules are an aid to interpreting the principles into practical applications and are intended to guide the ethical conduct of internal auditors.

Practice Advisory 1210-1: Proficiency

Interpretation of *Standard 1210* from the *International Standards for the Professional Practice of Internal Auditing*

Related Standard
1210 – Proficiency
Internal auditors should possess the knowledge, skills, and other competencies needed to perform their individual responsibilities. The internal audit activity collectively should possess or obtain the knowledge, skills, and other competencies needed to perform its responsibilities.

Nature of this Practice Advisory: Internal auditors should consider the following suggestions when evaluating proficiency. This guidance is not intended to represent all the considerations that may be necessary during such an evaluation, but simply a recommended set of items that should be addressed.

1. Each internal auditor should possess certain knowledge, skills, and other competencies:
    *   Proficiency in applying internal audit standards, procedures, and techniques is required in performing engagements. Proficiency means the ability to apply knowledge to situations likely to be encountered and to deal with them without extensive recourse to technical research and assistance.
    *   Proficiency in accounting principles and techniques is required of auditors who work extensively with financial records and reports.

- An understanding of management principles is required to recognize and evaluate the materiality and significance of deviations from good business practices. An understanding means the ability to apply broad knowledge to situations likely to be encountered, to recognize significant deviations, and to be able to carry out the research necessary to arrive at reasonable solutions.

- An appreciation is required of the fundamentals of subjects such as accounting, economics, commercial law, taxation, finance, quantitative methods, and information technology. An appreciation means the ability to recognize the existence of problems or potential problems and to determine the further research to be undertaken or the assistance to be obtained.

2. Internal auditors should be skilled in dealing with people and in communicating effectively. Internal auditors should understand human relations and maintain satisfactory relationships with engagement clients.

3. Internal auditors should be skilled in oral and written communications so that they can clearly and effectively convey such matters as engagement objectives, evaluations, conclusions, and recommendations.

4. The chief audit executive (CAE) should establish suitable criteria of education and experience for filling internal audit positions, giving due consideration to scope of work and level of responsibility. Reasonable assurance should be obtained as to each prospective auditor's qualifications and proficiency.

5. The internal audit staff should collectively possess the knowledge and skills essential to the practice of the profession within the organization. An annual analysis of an audit department's knowledge and skill sets should be performed to help identify

areas of opportunity which can be addressed by Continuing Professional Development, recruiting, or co-sourcing.

6. Continuing Professional Development is essential to help ensure an audit staff remains proficient. See Practice Advisory 1230-1 for specifics related to Continuing Professional Development.

7. The CAE should obtain assistance from experts outside the internal audit activity to support or complement areas where the activity is not fully proficient. See Practice Advisory 1210.A1-1 for more specifics related to obtaining services to support or complement the internal audit activity.

Practice Advisory 1210.A1-1: Obtaining Services to Support or Complement the Internal Audit Activity

Interpretation of *Standard 1210.A1* from the *International Standards for the Professional Practice of Internal Auditing*

> ***Related Standard***
> **1210.A1** – The chief audit executive should obtain competent advice and assistance if the internal audit staff lacks the knowledge, skills, or other competencies needed to perform all or part of the engagement.

Nature of this Practice Advisory: Internal auditors should consider the following suggestions when contemplating acquiring additional services to support the internal audit activity. This guidance is not intended to represent all the considerations that may be necessary, but simply a recommended set of items that should be addressed.

1. The internal audit activity should have employees or use outside service providers who are qualified in disciplines such as accounting, auditing, economics, finance, statistics, information technology, engineering, taxation, law, environmental affairs, and such other areas as needed to meet the internal audit activity's responsibilities. Each member of the internal audit activity, however, need not be qualified in all disciplines.

2. An outside service provider is a person or firm, independent of the organization, who has special knowledge, skill, and experience in a particular discipline. Outside service providers include, among others, actuaries, accountants, appraisers, environmental specialists, fraud investigators, lawyers, engineers, geologists, security specialists, statisticians, information technology specialists, the organization's external auditors, and other auditing organizations. An outside service provider may be engaged by the board, senior management, or the chief audit executive (CAE).

3. Outside service providers may be used by the internal audit activity in connection with, among other things:
    *   Audit activities where a specialized skill and knowledge are required such as information technology, statistics, taxes, language translations, or to achieve the objectives in the engagement work schedule.
    *   Valuations of assets such as land and buildings, works of art, precious gems, investments, and complex financial instruments.
    *   Determination of quantities or physical condition of certain assets such as mineral and petroleum reserves.
    *   Measuring the work completed and to be completed on contracts in progress.
    *   Fraud and security investigations.
    *   Determination of amounts by using specialized methods such as actuarial determinations of employee benefit obligations.
    *   Interpretation of legal, technical, and regulatory requirements.
    *   Evaluating the internal audit activity's quality improvement program in accordance with Section 1300 of the *International Standards for the Professional Practice of Internal Auditing (Standards)*.
    *   Mergers and acquisitions.
    *   Consulting on risk management and other matters.

4. When the CAE intends to use and rely on the work of an outside service provider, the CAE should assess the competency, independence, and objectivity of the outside service provider as it relates to the particular assignment to be performed. This assessment should also be made when the outside service provider is selected by senior management or the board, and the CAE intends to use and rely on the outside service provider's work. When the selection is made by others and the CAE's assessment determines that he or she should not use and rely on the work of an outside service provider, the results of the assessment should be communicated to senior management or the board, as appropriate.

5. The CAE should determine that the outside service provider possesses the necessary knowledge, skills, and other competencies to perform the engagement. When assessing competency, the CAE should consider:
   - Professional certification, license, or other recognition of the outside service provider's competency in the relevant discipline.
   - Membership of the outside service provider in an appropriate professional organization and adherence to that organization's code of ethics.
   - The reputation of the outside service provider. This may include contacting others familiar with the outside service provider's work.
   - The outside service provider's experience in the type of work being considered.
   - The extent of education and training received by the outside service provider in disciplines that pertain to the particular engagement.
   - The outside service provider's knowledge and experience in the industry in which the organization operates.

6. The CAE should assess the relationship of the outside service provider to the organization and to the internal audit activity to ensure that independence and objectivity are maintained throughout the engagement. In performing the assessment, the CAE should determine that there are no financial, organizational, or personal relationships that will prevent the outside service provider from rendering impartial and unbiased judgments and opinions when performing or reporting on the engagement.

7. In assessing the independence and objectivity of the outside service provider, the CAE should consider:
    *   The financial interest the provider may have in the organization.
    *   The personal or professional affiliation the provider may have to the board, senior management, or others within the organization.
    *   The relationship the provider may have had with the organization or the activities being reviewed.
    *   The extent of other ongoing services the provider may be performing for the organization.
    *   Compensation or other incentives that the provider may have.

8. If the outside service provider is also the organization's external auditor and the nature of the engagement is extended audit services, the CAE should ascertain that work performed does not impair the external auditor's independence. Extended audit services refers to those services beyond the requirements of audit standards generally accepted by external auditors. If the organization's external auditors act or appear to act as members of senior management, management, or as employees of the organization, then their independence is impaired. Additionally, external auditors may provide the organization with other services such as tax and consulting. Independence, however, should be assessed in relation to the full range of services provided to the organization.

9. The CAE should obtain sufficient information regarding the scope of the outside service provider's work. This is necessary in order to ascertain that the scope of work is adequate for the purposes of the internal audit activity. It may be prudent to have these and other matters documented in an engagement letter or contract. The CAE should review with the outside service provider:
    *   Objectives and scope of work.
    *   Specific matters expected to be covered in the engagement communications.
    *   Access to relevant records, personnel, and physical properties.
    *   Information regarding assumptions and procedures to be employed.
    *   Ownership and custody of engagement working papers, if applicable.
    *   Confidentiality and restrictions on information obtained during the engagement.
    *   Where applicable, compliance with The IIA's *Standards* and the audit department's standards for working practices should be referenced in the engagement letter.

10. Where the outside service provider performs internal audit activities, the CAE should specify and ensure that the work complies with the *Standards* and the audit department's standards for working practices. In reviewing the work of an outside service provider, the CAE should evaluate the adequacy of work performed. This evaluation should include sufficiency of information obtained to afford a reasonable basis for the conclusions reached and the resolution of significant exceptions or other unusual matters.

11. When the CAE issues engagement communications, and an outside service provider was used, the CAE may, as appropriate, refer to such services provided. The outside service provider

should be informed and, if appropriate, concurrence should be obtained prior to such reference being made in engagement communications.

Practice Advisory 1210.A2-1: Identification of Fraud

Interpretation of *Standard 1210.A2* from the *International Standards for the Professional Practice of Internal Auditing*

> *Related Standard*
> **1210.A2** – The internal auditor should have sufficient knowledge to identify the indicators of fraud but is not expected to have the expertise of a person whose primary responsibility is detecting and investigating fraud.

Nature of this Practice Advisory: Internal auditors should consider the following suggestions in connection with the identification of fraud. This guidance is not intended to represent all the considerations that may be necessary, but simply a recommended set of items that should be addressed.

1. Fraud encompasses an array of irregularities and illegal acts characterized by intentional deception. It can be perpetrated for the benefit of or to the detriment of the organization and by persons outside as well as inside the organization.

2. Fraud designed to benefit the organization generally produces such benefit by exploiting an unfair or dishonest advantage that also may deceive an outside party. Perpetrators of such frauds usually accrue an indirect personal benefit. Examples of frauds designed to benefit the organization include:

- Sale or assignment of fictitious or misrepresented assets.
- Improper payments such as illegal political contributions, bribes, kickbacks, and payoffs to government officials, intermediaries of government officials, customers, or suppliers.
- Intentional, improper representation or valuation of transactions, assets, liabilities, or income.
- Intentional, improper transfer pricing (e.g., valuation of goods exchanged between related organizations). By purposely structuring pricing techniques improperly, management can improve the operating results of an organization involved in the transaction to the detriment of the other organization.
- Intentional, improper related-party transactions in which one party receives some benefit not obtainable in an arm's-length transaction.
- Intentional failure to record or disclose significant information to improve the financial picture of the organization to outside parties.
- Prohibited business activities such as those that violate government statutes, rules, regulations, or contracts.
- Tax fraud.

3. Fraud perpetrated to the detriment of the organization generally is for the direct or indirect benefit of an employee, outside individual, or another organization. Some examples are:
   - Acceptance of bribes or kickbacks.
   - Diversion to an employee or outsider of a potentially profitable transaction that would normally generate profits for the organization.
   - Embezzlement, as typified by the misappropriation of money or property, and falsification of financial records to cover up the act, thus making detection difficult.
   - Intentional concealment or misrepresentation of events or data.

- Claims submitted for services or goods not actually provided to the organization.

4. Deterrence of fraud consists of those actions taken to discourage the perpetration of fraud and limit the exposure if fraud does occur. The principal mechanism for deterring fraud is control. Primary responsibility for establishing and maintaining control rests with management.

5. Internal auditors are responsible for assisting in the deterrence of fraud by examining and evaluating the adequacy and the effectiveness of the system of internal control, commensurate with the extent of the potential exposure/risk in the various segments of the organization's operations. In carrying out this responsibility, internal auditors should, for example, determine whether:
   - The organizational environment fosters control consciousness.
   - Realistic organizational goals and objectives are set.
   - Written policies (e.g., code of conduct) exist that describe prohibited activities and the action required whenever violations are discovered.
   - Appropriate authorization policies for transactions are established and maintained.
   - Policies, practices, procedures, reports, and other mechanisms are developed to monitor activities and safeguard assets, particularly in high-risk areas.
   - Communication channels provide management with adequate and reliable information.
   - Recommendations need to be made for the establishment or enhancement of cost-effective controls to help deter fraud.

6.   When an internal auditor suspects wrongdoing, the appropriate authorities within the organization should be informed. The internal auditor may recommend whatever investigation is considered necessary in the circumstances. Thereafter, the auditor should follow up to see that the internal audit activity's responsibilities have been met.

7.   Investigation of fraud consists of performing extended procedures necessary to determine whether fraud, as suggested by the indicators, has occurred. It includes gathering sufficient information about the specific details of a discovered fraud. Internal auditors, lawyers, investigators, security personnel, and other specialists from inside or outside the organization are the parties that usually conduct or participate in fraud investigations.

8.   When conducting fraud investigations, internal auditors should:
   •   Assess the probable level and the extent of complicity in the fraud within the organization. This can be critical to ensuring that the internal auditor avoids providing information to or obtaining misleading information from persons who may be involved.
   •   Determine the knowledge, skills, and other competencies needed to carry out the investigation effectively. An assessment of the qualifications and the skills of internal auditors and of the specialists available to participate in the investigation should be performed to ensure that engagements are conducted by individuals having appropriate types and levels of technical expertise. This should include assurances on such matters as professional certifications, licenses, reputation, and the fact that there is no relationship to those being investigated or to any of the employees or management of the organization.
   •   Design procedures to follow in attempting to identify the perpetrators, extent of the fraud, techniques used, and cause of the fraud.

- Coordinate activities with management personnel, legal counsel, and other specialists as appropriate throughout the course of the investigation.
- Be cognizant of the rights of alleged perpetrators and personnel within the scope of the investigation and the reputation of the organization itself.

9. Once a fraud investigation is concluded, internal auditors should assess the facts known in order to:
    - Determine if controls need to be implemented or strengthened to reduce future vulnerability.
    - Design engagement tests to help disclose the existence of similar frauds in the future.
    - Help meet the internal auditor's responsibility to maintain sufficient knowledge of fraud and thereby be able to identify future indicators of fraud.

10. Reporting of fraud consists of the various oral or written, interim or final communications to management regarding the status and results of fraud investigations. The chief audit executive has the responsibility to report immediately any incident of significant fraud to senior management and the board. Sufficient investigation should take place to establish reasonable certainty that a fraud has occurred before any fraud reporting is made. A preliminary or final report may be desirable at the conclusion of the detection phase. The report should include the internal auditor's conclusion as to whether sufficient information exists to conduct a full investigation. It should also summarize observations and recommendations that serve as the basis for such decision. A written report may follow any oral briefing made to management and the board to document the findings.

11. Section 2400 of the *International Standards for the Professional Practice of Internal Auditing (Standards)* provides interpretations applicable to engagement

communications issued as a result of fraud investigations. Additional interpretive guidance on reporting of fraud is as follows:

- When the incidence of significant fraud has been established to a reasonable certainty, senior management and the board should be notified immediately.
- The results of a fraud investigation may indicate that fraud has had a previously undiscovered significant adverse effect on the financial position and results of operations of an organization for one or more years on which financial statements have already been issued. Internal auditors should inform senior management and the board of such a discovery.
- A written report or other formal communication should be issued at the conclusion of the investigation phase. It should include all observations, conclusions, recommendations, and corrective action taken.
- A draft of the proposed final communications on fraud should be submitted to legal counsel for review. In those cases in which the internal auditor wants to invoke client privilege, consideration should be given to addressing the report to legal counsel.

12. Detection of fraud consists of identifying indicators of fraud sufficient to warrant recommending an investigation. These indicators may arise as a result of controls established by management, tests conducted by auditors, and other sources both within and outside the organization.

13. In conducting engagements, the internal auditor's responsibilities for detecting fraud are to:
- Have sufficient knowledge of fraud to be able to identify indicators that fraud may have been committed. This knowledge includes the characteristics of fraud, the techniques used to commit fraud, and the types of fraud associated with the activities reviewed.

- Be alert to opportunities, such as control weaknesses, that could allow fraud. If significant control weaknesses are detected, additional tests conducted by internal auditors should include tests directed toward identification of other indicators of fraud. Some examples of indicators are unauthorized transactions, override of controls, unexplained pricing exceptions, and unusually large product losses. Internal auditors should recognize that the presence of more than one indicator at any one time increases the probability that fraud may have occurred.
- Evaluate the indicators that fraud may have been committed and decide whether any further action is necessary or whether an investigation should be recommended.
- Notify the appropriate authorities within the organization if a determination is made that there are sufficient indicators of the commission of a fraud to recommend an investigation.

14. Internal auditors are not expected to have knowledge equivalent to that of a person whose primary responsibility is detecting and investigating fraud. Also, audit procedures alone, even when carried out with due professional care, do not guarantee that fraud will be detected.

Practice Advisory 1210.A2-2: Responsibility for Fraud Detection

Interpretation of *Standard 1210.A2* from the *International Standards for the Professional Practice of Internal Auditing*

> *Related Standard*
> **1210.A2** – The internal auditor should have sufficient knowledge to identify the indicators of fraud but is not expected to have the expertise of a person whose primary responsibility is detecting and investigating fraud.

Nature of this Practice Advisory: Internal auditors should consider the following suggestions in relation to the responsibility for fraud detection. This guidance is not intended to represent all the considerations that may be necessary, but simply a recommended set of items that should be addressed.

1. Management and the internal audit activity have differing roles with respect to fraud detection. The normal course of work for the internal audit activity is to provide an independent appraisal, examination, and evaluation of an organization's activities as a service to the organization. The objective of internal auditing in fraud detection is to assist members of the organization in the effective discharge of their responsibilities by furnishing them with analyses, appraisals, recommendations, counsel, and information concerning the activities reviewed. The engagement objective includes promoting effective control at a reasonable cost.

2. Management has a responsibility to establish and maintain an effective control system at a reasonable cost. To the degree that fraud may be present in activities covered in the normal course of work as defined above, internal auditors have a responsibility to exercise "due professional care" as specifically defined in *Standard 1220* with respect to fraud detection. Internal auditors should have sufficient knowledge of fraud to identify the indicators that fraud may have been committed, be alert to opportunities that could allow fraud, evaluate the need for additional investigation, and notify the appropriate authorities.

3. A well-designed internal control system should not be conducive to fraud. Tests conducted by auditors, along with reasonable controls established by management, improve the likelihood that any existing fraud indicators will be detected and considered for further investigation.

Practice Advisory 1220-1: Due Professional Care

Interpretation of *Standard 1220* from the *International Standards for the Professional Practice of Internal Auditing*

Related Standard
1220 – Due Professional Care
Internal auditors should apply the care and skill expected of a reasonably prudent and competent internal auditor. Due professional care does not imply infallibility.

Nature of this Practice Advisory: Internal auditors should consider the following suggestions when evaluating due professional care. This guidance is not intended to represent all the considerations that may be necessary during such an evaluation, but simply a recommended set of items that should be addressed.

1. Due professional care calls for the application of the care and skill expected of a reasonably prudent and competent internal auditor in the same or similar circumstances. Professional care should, therefore, be appropriate to the complexities of the engagement being performed. In exercising due professional care, internal auditors should be alert to the possibility of intentional wrongdoing, errors and omissions, inefficiency, waste, ineffectiveness, and conflicts of interest. They should also be alert to those conditions and activities where irregularities are most likely to occur. In addition, they should identify inadequate

controls and recommend improvements to promote compliance with acceptable procedures and practices.

2. Due care implies reasonable care and competence, not infallibility or extraordinary performance. Due care requires the auditor to conduct examinations and verifications to a reasonable extent, but does not require detailed reviews of all transactions. Accordingly, internal auditors cannot give absolute assurance that noncompliance or irregularities do not exist. Nevertheless, the possibility of material irregularities or noncompliance should be considered whenever an internal auditor undertakes an internal auditing assignment.

Practice Advisory 1230-1:
Continuing Professional Development

Interpretation of *Standard 1230* from the
International Standards for the
Professional Practice of Internal Auditing

Related Standard
1230 – Continuing Professional Development
Internal auditors should enhance their knowledge, skills, and other
competencies through continuing professional development.

Nature of this Practice Advisory: Internal auditors should
consider the following suggestions in connection with continuing
professional development. This guidance is not intended to
represent all the considerations that may be necessary during
such an evaluation, but simply a recommended set of items that
should be addressed.

1. Internal auditors are responsible for continuing their education
    in order to maintain their proficiency. They should keep informed
    about improvements and current developments in internal audit
    standards, procedures, and techniques. Continuing education
    may be obtained through membership and participation in
    professional societies; attendance at conferences, seminars,
    college courses, and in-house training programs; and participation
    in research projects.

2. Internal auditors are encouraged to demonstrate their proficiency
    by obtaining appropriate professional certification, such as the

Certified Internal Auditor designation and other designations offered by The Institute of Internal Auditors (IIA).

3. Internal auditors with professional certifications should obtain sufficient continuing professional education to satisfy requirements related to the professional certification held.

4. Internal auditors not presently holding appropriate certifications are encouraged to pursue an educational program that supports efforts to obtain professional certification.

Practice Advisory 1300-1: Quality Assurance and Improvement Program

Interpretation of *Standard 1300* from the
International Standards for the
Professional Practice of Internal Auditing

Related Standard
1300 – Quality Assurance and Improvement Program
The chief audit executive should develop and maintain a quality assurance and improvement program that covers all aspects of the internal audit activity and continuously monitors its effectiveness. This program includes periodic internal and external quality assessments and ongoing internal monitoring. Each part of the program should be designed to help the internal auditing activity add value and improve the organization's operations and to provide assurance that the internal audit activity is in conformity with the *Standards* and the Code of Ethics.

Nature of this Practice Advisory: Internal auditors should consider the following suggestions when developing or assessing quality programs. This guidance is not intended to represent all the procedures necessary for comprehensive quality programs or their assessment, but simply a recommended set of quality assessment practices.

1. **Overview of a Quality Assurance and Improvement Program (QA&IP)** — The chief audit executive (CAE) is

responsible for establishing an internal audit activity whose scope of work includes all the activities in the *International Standards for the Professional Practice of Internal Auditing (Standards)* and in The Institute of Internal Auditor's (IIA) definition of internal auditing. To ensure that this occurs, *Standard 1300* requires that the CAE develop and maintain a quality assurance and improvement program (QA&IP).

2. **Implementing a QA&IP** — The CAE should be accountable for implementing processes that are designed to provide reasonable assurance to the various stakeholders of the internal audit activity that it:
   - Performs in accordance with its charter, which should be consistent with the *Standards* and Code of Ethics,
   - Operates in an effective and efficient manner, and
   - Is perceived by those stakeholders as adding value and improving the organization's operations.

   These processes should include appropriate supervision, periodic internal assessments and ongoing monitoring of quality assurance, and periodic external assessments.

3. **Nature and Scope of a QA&IP** — The QA&IP should be sufficiently comprehensive to encompass all aspects of operation and management of an internal audit activity, as found in the *Standards* and best practices of the profession. The QA&IP processes should be performed by or under direct supervision of the CAE. Except in small internal audit activities, the CAE would usually delegate most QA&IP responsibilities to subordinates. In large or complex environments (e.g., numerous business units and/or locations), the CAE should establish a formal QA&IP function independent of the audit and consulting segments of the internal audit activity. This independent function should be headed by an audit executive. This executive (and limited staff) would not normally perform all of the QA&IP responsibilities, but would administer and monitor these activities.

4. **Key Elements of a QA&IP** — The QA&IP should be structured to achieve an optimum level of professional competence and reviews should be administered, to the extent practicable, independently of the functions and activities being reviewed. The following key elements of the internal audit activity — performed by, or administered by a person or functional unit under the direction of, the CAE — should be considered for the QA&IP function:

- Oversee the development and implementation of internal audit policies/procedures; administer/maintain the internal audit activity's policy/procedure manual.
- Assist the CAE and audit management with budgeting and financial administration for the internal audit activity.
- Maintain and update the comprehensive audit risk universe, including gathering and incorporating new information impacting the universe; overseeing the division of responsibilities among internal audit, external audit, and other evaluation and investigation functions.
- Administer the general operation of the system for evaluation of audit risk and long-range planning — assisting the CAE and audit management in this area.
- Assist with the overall scheduling process for audit and consulting engagements and the associated time tracking.
- Assist internal audit management in the acquisition, maintenance, and employment of audit tools and other use of technology.
- Administer external recruitment and the internal audit activity's participation in the organization's internal staff rotation and management development programs.
- Oversee the training/development of staff — e.g., selection or development of training courses, and administration of the related career planning and performance evaluation processes, including the tracking system for professional development of individual staff members.

- Oversee the system(s) for internal audit statistics/metrics and for post-audit and other surveys (e.g., of the customers and other stakeholders of the internal audit activity).
- Administer/monitor quality assurance and process improvement activities, including formal internal and external quality assessments.
- Oversee/administer information gathering and preparation of the periodic summary reports by the internal audit activity to senior management and the audit committee (including reports of the results of internal and external quality assessments).
- Administer/maintain the comprehensive follow-up database for recommendations and action plans resulting from internal audit engagements and the work of external auditors and other internal evaluation and investigation functions.
- Assist the CAE, audit management, and internal audit staff in keeping current with the *Standards*, other changes and emerging best practices of the internal audit profession, regulatory matters, and other emerging issues and opportunities — under the direction of internal audit management.
- The words "assist, administer, oversee, monitor, and maintain" are intended to indicate that the person(s) working in the QA&IP function would not necessarily perform much of this work. It would be assigned — either ad-hoc for particular tasks or on a longer-term basis — to other internal audit executives and staff, but would be overseen, administered, etc. through the QA&IP.

Practice Advisory 1310-1: Quality Program Assessments

Interpretation of *Standard 1310* from the *International Standards for the Professional Practice of Internal Auditing*

Related Standard
1310 – Quality Program Assessments
The internal audit activity should adopt a process to monitor and assess the overall effectiveness of the quality program. The process should include both internal and external assessments.

Nature of this Practice Advisory: Internal auditors should consider the following suggestions when developing or assessing quality programs. This guidance is not intended to represent all the procedures necessary for comprehensive quality programs or their assessment, but simply a recommended set of quality assessment practices.

1. **Monitoring Quality Programs** — Means ongoing and periodic assessments of the entire spectrum of audit and consulting work performed by the internal audit activity, and is not limited to assessing its Quality Assurance and Improvement Program (QA&IP) — see Practice Advisory 1300-1. These ongoing and periodic assessments should be comprised of rigorous, comprehensive processes, both routine, continuous supervision and testing of performance of audit and consulting work, and periodic validations of compliance with the *International Standards for the Professional Practice of Internal Auditing*

(Standards). Monitoring should also include ongoing measurements and analyses of performance metrics (e.g., audit plan accomplishment, cycle time, recommendations accepted, and customer satisfaction). If the results of these assessments indicate areas for improvement by the internal audit activity, the improvements should be implemented by the chief audit executive (CAE) through the QA&IP.

2. **Definition and Timing of Assessments**
   - Ongoing internal assessments (the term "internal assessments" is synonymous with the terms "internal review" and "self-assessment" used elsewhere in the Practice Advisories) should be an integral part of the day-to-day supervision, review, and measurement of the internal audit activity, as set forth in Practice Advisory 1311-1, Paragraphs 2 and 3.
   - Periodic internal assessments should be completed as set forth in Practice Advisory 1311-1, Paragraphs 4 and 5.
   - Periodic external assessments of the internal audit activity, by an individual or team having a high level of competence and experience in the internal audit profession, should be performed in accordance with Practice Advisories 1312-1 and 1312-2 (New).
   - The requirement that internal audit activities conduct ongoing and periodic internal assessments became effective as of January 1, 2002. In addition, at least one external assessment is required during the five years commencing on that date and at least once during each five-year period thereafter. The requirement for a periodic internal assessment may be waived for the year in which an external assessment is performed.

3. **Assessing Quality Programs** — Assessments should evaluate and conclude on the quality of the internal audit activity and lead to recommendations for appropriate improvements. Assessments of quality programs should include evaluation of:

   - Compliance with the *Standards* and Code of Ethics, including timely corrective actions to remedy any significant instances of noncompliance,
   - Adequacy of the internal audit activity's charter, goals, objectives, policies, and procedures,
   - Contribution to the organization's governance, risk management, and control processes,
   - Compliance with applicable laws, regulations, and government or industry standards,
   - Effectiveness of continuous improvement activities and adoption of best practices, and
   - Whether the auditing activity adds value and improves the organization's operations.

4. **Continuous Improvement** — All quality assessment and improvement efforts should include appropriate, timely modification of resources, technology, processes, and procedures as indicated by monitoring and assessment activities.

5. **Communicating Results** — To provide accountability and transparency, the CAE should share the results of external, and, as appropriate, internal quality program assessments with the various stakeholders of the activity, such as senior management, the board, and external auditors.

Practice Advisory 1311-1: Internal Assessments

**Interpretation of *Standard 1311* from the
*International Standards for the
Professional Practice of Internal Auditing***

Related Standard
1311 – Internal Assessments
Internal assessments should include:
- Ongoing reviews of the performance of the internal audit activity; and
- Periodic reviews performed through self-assessment or by other persons within the organization with knowledge of internal auditing practices and the *Standards*.

Nature of this Practice Advisory: Internal auditors should consider these suggestions when performing internal assessments within the internal audit activity. This guidance is not intended to represent all the procedures necessary for comprehensive internal assessments, but simply a recommended set of internal assessment practices.

1. **Overview of a Quality Assurance and Improvement Program (QA&IP)** — The chief audit executive (CAE) is responsible for establishing an internal audit activity whose scope of work includes all the activities in the *International Standards for the Professional Practice of Internal Auditing (Standards)* and in The Institute of Internal Auditor's (IIA) definition of internal auditing. To ensure that this occurs, *Standard*

1300 requires that the CAE develop and maintain a Quality Assurance and Improvement Program (QA&IP). The QA&IP should include both ongoing and periodic internal assessments (the term "internal assessments" is synonymous with the terms "internal review" and "self-assessment" used elsewhere in the Practice Advisories). These ongoing and periodic assessments should cover the entire spectrum of audit and consulting work performed by the internal audit activity and should not be limited to assessing its QA&IP — see Practice Advisory 1300-1.

2. **Ongoing Internal Assessments** — Are usually incorporated into the routine policies and practices used to manage the internal audit activity and should be conducted by means of such processes and tools as:
    - Engagement supervision as described in Practice Advisory 2340-1, Engagement Supervision,
    - Checklists and other means to provide assurance that processes adopted by the internal audit activity (e.g., in an audit and procedures manual) are being followed,
    - Feedback from audit customers and other stakeholders,
    - Project budgets, timekeeping systems, audit plan completion, cost recoveries, and
    - Analyses of other performance metrics (such as cycle time and recommendations accepted).

3. Conclusions should be developed as to the quality of ongoing performance, and follow-up action should be taken to assure appropriate improvements are implemented.

4. **Periodic Internal Assessments** — Usually represent non-routine, special-purpose reviews and compliance testing. They should be designed to assess (a) compliance with the internal audit activity's charter, the *Standards,* and the Code of Ethics, and (b) the efficiency and effectiveness of the activity in meeting the needs of its various stakeholders. The IIA's *Quality*

Assessment Manual, or a comparable set of guidance and tools, should serve as the basis for periodic internal assessments.

5. Periodic Assessments May:
    *   Include more in-depth interviews and surveys of stakeholder groups,
    *   Be performed by members of the internal audit activity (self-assessment),
    *   Be performed by Certified Internal Auditors (CIAs), or other competent audit professionals, currently assigned elsewhere in the organization,
    *   *Encompass a combination of self-assessment and preparation of materials subsequently reviewed by CIAs, or other competent audit professionals, and*
    *   Include benchmarking of the internal audit activity's practices and performance metrics against relevant best practices of the internal auditing profession.

6. A periodic internal assessment performed within a short time prior to an external assessment can serve to facilitate and reduce the cost of an external assessment. If the external assessment takes the form of a "self-assessment with independent validation" (New Practice Advisory 1312-2), the periodic internal assessment can serve as the self-assessment portion of this process.

7. Conclusions should be developed as to the quality of performance and appropriate action initiated to achieve improvements and conformity to the *Standards,* as necessary.

8. The CAE should establish a structure for reporting results of periodic reviews that maintains appropriate credibility and objectivity. Generally, those assigned responsibility for conducting ongoing and periodic reviews should report to the CAE while performing the reviews and should communicate their results directly to the CAE.

9. **Communicating Results** — The CAE should share the results of internal assessments, necessary action plans, and their successful implementation with appropriate persons outside the activity, such as senior management, the board, and external auditors.

Practice Advisory 1312-1:
External Assessments

**Interpretation of *Standard 1312* from the
*International Standards for the
Professional Practice of Internal Auditing***

> ***Related Standard***
> **1312 – External Assessments**
> *External assessments, such as quality assurance reviews,
> should be conducted at least once every five years by a
> qualified, independent reviewer or review team from outside
> the organization.*

*Nature of this Practice Advisory: Internal auditors should
consider these suggestions when planning and contracting for
an external assessment of their internal audit activity. This
guidance is not intended to represent all the considerations
necessary for an external assessment but simply a recommended
set of high-level considerations with respect to the external
assessment.*

1. **Overview of a Quality Assurance and Improvement
   Program (QA&IP)** — The chief audit executive (CAE) is
   responsible for establishing an internal audit activity whose scope
   of work includes all the activities in the *International Standards
   for the Professional Practice of Internal Auditing
   (Standards)* and in The Institute of Internal Auditor's (IIA)
   definition of internal auditing. To ensure that this occurs, *Standard
   1300* requires that the CAE develop and maintain a Quality
   Assurance and Improvement Program (QA&IP). The QA&IP

should include a periodic external assessment, conducted at least once every five years by a qualified, independent reviewer or review team. These external assessments should cover the entire spectrum of audit and consulting work performed by the internal audit activity and should not be limited to assessing its QA&IP — see Practice Advisory 1300-1.

2. **General Considerations** — External assessments of an internal audit activity should appraise and express an opinion as to the internal audit activity's compliance with the *Standards* and, as appropriate, should include recommendations for improvement. These reviews can have considerable value to the CAE and other members of the internal audit activity. Only qualified persons (Paragraph 5., below) should perform such reviews.

3. An external assessment is required within five years of January 1, 2002. <u>Earlier adoption of the new Standard requiring an external review is highly recommended.</u> Organizations that have had external reviews prior to that date are encouraged to have their next external review within five years of their last review.

4. On completion of the review, a formal communication should be provided to the board (as defined in the Glossary to the *Standards*) and to senior management.

5. **Qualifications for External Reviewers** — External reviewers, including those who validate self-assessments (New Practice Advisory 1312-2), should be independent of the organization and of the internal audit activity. The review team should consist of individuals who are competent in the professional practice of internal auditing and the external assessment process. To be considered as candidates to be external assessors, qualified individuals could include IIA quality assurance reviewers, regulatory examiners, consultants, external

auditors, other professional service providers, and internal auditors from outside the organization whose internal audit activity is the subject of the external assessment.

6. **Independence** — The individual or organization that undertakes to perform the external assessment, the members of the assessment team, and any other individuals who participate in the assessment should be free from any obligation to, or interest in, the organization whose internal audit activity is the subject of the external assessment or the personnel of such organization. Particular considerations relating to independence of external assessors include:

   - Individuals who perform the assessment must be independent of the organization whose internal audit activity is the subject of the assessment and must not have either a real or an apparent conflict of interest. "Independent of the organization" means not a part of, or under the control of, the organization to which the internal auditing activity belongs. In the selection of an external reviewer, consideration should be given to a possible real or apparent conflict of interest that the reviewer may have due to present or past relationships with the organization or its internal auditing activity.

   - Individuals who are in another department of that subject organization or in a related organization, although organizationally separate from the internal audit activity, are not considered independent for purposes of conducting an external assessment. A "related organization" may be a parent organization, an affiliate in the same group of entities, or an entity with regular oversight, supervision, or quality assurance responsibilities with respect to the organization whose internal audit activity is the subject of the external assessment.

   - Reciprocal peer review arrangements between three or more organizations (e.g., within an industry or other affinity group, regional association, or other group of organizations) may be structured in a manner that alleviates independence concerns, but care must be taken to ensure that the issue of independence does not arise. Reciprocal peer reviews between two organizations would not pass the independence test.

- To overcome concerns that there may be an appearance or reality of impairment of independence in instances such as those discussed in this paragraph, one or more independent individuals could be part of the external assessment team, or scheduled to participate subsequently, to independently validate the work of that external assessment team.

7. **Integrity and Objectivity** — *Integrity* requires the review team to be honest and candid within the constraints of confidentiality. Service and the public trust should not be subordinated to personal gain and advantage. *Objectivity* is a state of mind and a quality that lends value to a review team's services. The principle of objectivity imposes the obligation to be impartial, intellectually honest, and free of conflicts of interest.

8. **Competence** — Performing and communicating the results of an external assessment require the exercise of professional judgment. Accordingly, an individual serving as an external assessor should:

- Be a competent, certified audit professional (e.g., CIA, CPA, CA, or CISA) who possesses current, in-depth knowledge of the *Standards*.
- Be well versed in the best practices of the profession.
- Have at least three years of recent experience in the practice of internal auditing at a management level.
- External assessment team leaders and independent validators (New Practice Advisory 1312-2) should have an additional level of competence and experience, such as that gained from working previously as a team member on an external

quality assessment, successful completion of The IIA's quality assessment training course or similar training, and CAE or comparable senior internal audit management experience.

9. The review team should include members with information technology expertise and relevant industry experience. Individuals with expertise in other specialized areas may assist the external review team. For example, specialists in enterprise risk management, statistical sampling, operations monitoring systems, or control self-assessment may participate in certain segments of the review.

10. **Approval by Management and the Board** — The CAE should involve senior management and the board in the selection process for an external reviewer and obtain their approval.

11. **Scope of External Assessments** — The external assessment should consist of a broad scope of coverage that includes the following elements of the internal audit activity:
   - Compliance with the *Standards*, The IIA's Code of Ethics, and the internal audit activity's charter, plans, policies, procedures, practices, and applicable legislative and regulatory requirements,
   - Expectations of the internal audit activity expressed by the board, executive management, and operational managers,
   - Integration of the internal audit activity into the organization's governance process, including the attendant relationships between and among the key groups involved in that process,
   - Tools and techniques employed by the internal audit activity,
   - Mix of knowledge, experience, and disciplines within the staff, including staff focus on process improvement, and
   - Determination as to whether or not the audit activity adds value and improves the organization's operations.

12. **Communicating Results** — The preliminary results of the review should be discussed with the CAE during and at the conclusion of the assessment process. Final results should be communicated to the CAE or other official who authorized the review for the organization, preferably with copies sent directly to appropriate members of senior management and the board.

13. The communication should include the following:
    - An opinion on the internal audit activity's compliance with the *Standards* based on a structured rating process. The term "compliance" means that the practices of the internal audit activity, taken as a whole, satisfy the requirements of the *Standards*. Similarly, "noncompliance" means that the impact and severity of the deficiencies in the practices of the internal audit activity are so significant that they impair the internal audit activity's ability to discharge its responsibilities. The degree of "partial compliance" with individual *Standards*, if relevant to the overall opinion, should also be expressed in the report on the independent assessment. The expression of an opinion on the results of the external assessment requires the application of sound business judgment, integrity, and due professional care.
    - An assessment and evaluation of the use of best practices, both those observed during the assessment and others potentially applicable to the activity.
    - Recommendations for improvement, where appropriate.
    - Responses from the CAE that include an action plan and implementation dates.

14. The CAE should communicate the results of the review to appropriate members of senior management and to the board, if not already copied directly, as well as the specifics of planned remedial actions for significant issues and subsequent information as to accomplishment of those planned actions.

Practice Advisory 1312-2:
External Assessments Self-assessment with Independent Validation

**Interpretation of *Standard 1312* from the
*International Standards for the
Professional Practice of Internal Auditing***

Related Standard
1312 – External Assessments
External assessments, such as quality assurance reviews, should be conducted at least once every five years by a qualified, independent reviewer or review team from outside the organization.

Nature of this Practice Advisory: Internal auditors should consider these suggestions when planning and contracting for an external assessment of their internal audit activity. This guidance is not intended to represent all the considerations necessary for an external assessment, but simply a recommended set of high-level considerations with respect to the external assessment.

1. **Overview of a Quality Assurance and Improvement Program (QA&IP)** — The chief audit executive (CAE) is responsible for establishing an internal audit activity whose scope of work includes all the activities in the *International Standards for the Professional Practice of Internal Auditing (Standards)* and in The Institute of Internal Auditor's (IIA) definition of internal auditing. To ensure that this occurs, *Standard 1300* requires that the CAE develop and maintain a Quality

Assurance and Improvement Program (QA&IP). The QA&IP should include a periodic external assessment conducted at least once every five years by a qualified, independent reviewer or review team. These external assessments should cover the entire spectrum of audit and consulting work performed by the internal audit activity and should not be limited to assessing its QA&IP — see Practice Advisory 1300-1.

2. **Self-assessment with Independent Validation** — In response to concerns that an external assessment by an independent individual or team may be onerous for smaller internal audit activities, The IIA has provided an alternative process, a "self-assessment with independent [external] validation," with the following features:

   - A comprehensive and fully documented self-assessment process, which should emulate the external assessment process, at least with respect to evaluation of compliance with the *Standards*.
   - An independent on-site validation by a qualified reviewer.
   - Economical time and resource requirements — e.g., the primary focus would be on compliance with the *Standards*. Attention to other areas such as benchmarking, review and consultation as to employment of best practices, and interviews with senior and operating management (whose views and concerns the CAE and staff of the internal audit activity already know) may be reduced or omitted.
   - Otherwise, the same requirements and criteria as set forth in Practice Advisory 1312-1 would apply for:
   - General considerations.
   - Qualifications of the independent validator (external reviewer).
   - Independence, integrity and objectivity, competence, approval by management and the board, scope (except for areas such as employment of tools, techniques, other best practices, career development, and value-adding activities).

- Communication of results (including remedial actions and their accomplishment).

3. A team under the direction of the CAE should perform and fully document the self-assessment process. The IIA's *Quality Assessment Manual* contains an outline of the process, including guidance and tools for the self-assessment. A draft report, similar to that for an external assessment, should be prepared.

4. A qualified, independent validator should perform limited tests of the self-assessment so as to validate the results and express an opinion about the indicated level of the activity's conformity to the *Standards*. This independent validation should follow the process outlined in The IIA's *Quality Assessment Manual* or a similar comprehensive process.

5. Upon completion of the independent validation, including a rigorous review of the self-assessment team's evaluation of compliance with the *Standards* and the Code of Ethics:
    - The independent validator should review the draft report mentioned in Paragraph 3., above, and attempt to reconcile unresolved issues (if any).
    - If in agreement with the evaluation of compliance with the *Standards* and Code of Ethics, the independent validator should add wording (as needed) to the report, concurring in the evaluation and, to the extent deemed appropriate, in the report's findings, conclusions, and recommendations.
    - If not in agreement with that evaluation, the independent evaluator should add dissenting wording to the report, specifying the points of disagreement with it and, to the extent deemed appropriate, with the significant findings, conclusions, and recommendations in the report.
    - Alternatively, the independent validator may prepare a separate independent validation report, concurring or

expressing disagreement as outlined above, to accompany the report of the self-assessment.

- The final report(s) of the self-assessment with independent validation should then be signed by the self-assessment team and the independent validator and issued by the CAE to senior management and the board.

6. While a full external review achieves maximum benefit for the activity and should be included in the activity's quality program, the self-assessment with independent validation provides an alternative means of complying fully with this Standard 1312. However, insofar as possible, in order to achieve optimum quality assurance and process-improvement benefits, an internal audit activity should consider the self-assessment with independent validation as an interim measure and endeavor to obtain a full external assessment during subsequent periods.

Practice Advisory 1320-1:
Reporting on the Quality Program

**Interpretation of *Standard 1320* from the
*International Standards for the
Professional Practice of Internal Auditing***

Related Standard
1320 – Reporting on the Quality Program
*The chief audit executive should communicate the results of
external assessments to the board.*

---

*Nature of this Practice Advisory: Internal auditors should
consider the following suggestions when reporting on the quality
program. This guidance is not intended to represent all the
considerations that may be necessary, but simply a recommended
set of items that should be addressed.*

1. Upon completion of an external assessment, the review team
    should issue a formal report containing an opinion on the internal
    audit activity's compliance with the *International Standards
    for the Professional Practice of Internal Auditing
    (Standards)* (see Practice Advisory 1312-1). The report should
    also address compliance with the internal audit activity's charter
    and other applicable standards and include appropriate
    recommendations for improvement. The report should be
    addressed to the person or organization requesting the
    assessment. The chief audit executive should prepare a written
    action plan in response to the significant comments and
    recommendations contained in the report of external assessment.

Appropriate follow-up is also the chief audit executive's responsibility.

2. The evaluation of compliance with the *Standards* is a critical component of an external assessment. The review team should acknowledge the *Standards* in order to evaluate and opine on the internal audit activity's compliance. However, as noted in Practice Advisory 1310-1, there are additional criteria that should be considered in evaluating the performance of an internal audit activity.

Practice Advisory 1330-1:
Use of "Conducted in Accordance
with the *Standards*"

**Interpretation of *Standard 1330* from the
*International Standards for the
Professional Practice of Internal Auditing***

Related Standard
**1330 – Use of "Conducted in Accordance with the
Standards"**
Internal auditors are encouraged to report that their activities
are "conducted in accordance with the *International Standards
for the Professional Practice of Internal Auditing*." However,
internal auditors may use the statement only if assessments of
the quality improvement program demonstrate that the internal
audit activity is in compliance with the *Standards*.

---

*Nature of this Practice Advisory: Internal auditors should
consider these suggestions when using the phrase "conducted
in accordance with the International Standards for the
Professional Practice of Internal Auditing." This guidance is
not intended to be all-inclusive, but simply to supplement the*
Standards.

1. **General Considerations** — External and internal assessments
   of an internal audit activity should be performed to appraise and
   express an opinion as to the internal audit activity's compliance
   with the *International Standards for the Professional Practice
   of Internal Auditing (Standards)* and the Code of Ethics and,

as appropriate, should include recommendations for improvement.

2. An external assessment is required within five years of January 1, 2002. Earlier adoption of the new standard requiring an external review is highly recommended. Organizations that have had external reviews are encouraged to have their next external review within five years of their last review.

3. **Use of Compliance Phrase** — The compliance phrase to be used may be: "in compliance with the *Standards,*" or "in conformity to the *Standards*," or "in accordance with the *Standards.*" Use of the compliance phrase requires an external assessment at least once during each five-year period, along with periodic internal assessments, which have concluded that the internal audit activity is in compliance with the *Standards* and Code of Ethics. Initial use of the compliance phrase is not appropriate until an external review, performed within the past five years, has demonstrated that the internal audit activity is in compliance with the *Standards* and the Code of Ethics. Instances of noncompliance that impact the overall scope or operation of the internal audit activity, including failure to obtain an external assessment by January 1, 2007, should be disclosed to senior management and the board.

4. Prior to the internal audit activity's use of the compliance phrase, any instances of noncompliance that have been disclosed by a quality assessment (internal or external), which impair the internal audit activity's ability to discharge its responsibilities:
   - Should be adequately remedied,
   - The remedial actions should be documented and reported to the relevant assessor(s), to obtain concurrence that the noncompliance has been adequately remedied, and
   - The remedial actions and agreement of the relevant assessor(s) therewith should be reported to senior management and the board.

Practice Advisory 2000-1:
Managing the Internal Audit Activity

**Interpretation of *Standard 2000* from the
*International Standards for the
Professional Practice of Internal Auditing***

Related Standard
2000 – Managing the Internal Audit Activity
The chief audit executive should effectively manage the internal
audit activity to ensure it adds value to the organization.

Nature of this Practice Advisory: *Internal auditors should
consider the following suggestions in connection with managing
the internal audit activity. This guidance is not intended to
represent all the considerations that may be necessary, but simply
a recommended set of items that should be addressed.*

1. The chief audit executive is responsible for properly managing
    the internal audit activity so that:
    *   Audit work fulfills the general purposes and responsibilities
        described in the charter, approved by the board, and senior
        management as appropriate.
    *   Resources of the internal audit activity are efficiently and
        effectively employed.
    *   Audit work conforms to the *International Standards for
        the Professional Practice of Internal Auditing
        (Standards)*.

Practice Advisory 2010-1: Planning

Interpretation of *Standard 2010* from the *International Standards for the Professional Practice of Internal Auditing*

> *Related Standard*
> **2010 – Planning**
> The chief audit executive should establish risk-based plans to determine the priorities of the internal audit activity, consistent with the organization's goals. The chief audit executive should establish risk-based plans to determine the priorities of the internal audit activity, consistent with the organization's goals.

Nature of this Practice Advisory: Internal auditors should consider the following suggestions when planning for the internal audit activity. This guidance is not intended to represent all the considerations that may be necessary, but simply a recommended set of items that should be addressed.

1. Planning for the internal audit activity should be consistent with its charter and with the goals of the organization. The planning process involves establishing:
   - Goals.
   - Engagement work schedules.
   - Staffing plans and financial budgets.
   - Activity reports.

2. The goals of the internal audit activity should be capable of being accomplished within specified operating plans and budgets and,

to the extent possible, should be measurable. They should be accompanied by measurement criteria and targeted dates of accomplishment.

3. Engagement work schedules should include:
    - What activities are to be performed;
    - When they will be performed; and
    - The estimated time required, taking into account the scope of the engagement work planned and the nature and extent of related work performed by others.

4. Matters to be considered in establishing engagement work schedule priorities should include:
    - The dates and results of the last engagement;
    - Updated assessments of risks and effectiveness of risk management and control processes;
    - Requests by the board and senior management;
    - Current issues relating to organizational governance;
    - Major changes in enterprise's business, operations, programs, systems, and controls;
    - Opportunities to achieve operating benefits; and
    - Changes to and capabilities of the audit staff. The work schedules should be sufficiently flexible to cover unanticipated demands on the internal audit activity.

Practice Advisory 2010-2: Linking the Audit Plan to Risk and Exposures

Interpretation of *Standard 2100* from the *International Standards for the Professional Practice of Internal Auditing*

Related Standard
2010 – Planning
The chief audit executive should establish risk-based plans to determine the priorities of the internal audit activity, consistent with the organization's goals.

Nature of this Practice Advisory: The organization's risk strategy should be reflected in the design of the internal audit activity's plan. A coordinated approach should be applied to leverage synergies between the organization's risk management and internal audit processes. Additional considerations beyond those contained in this advisory may be necessary.

1. Any organization faces a number of uncertainties and risks which can both negatively or positively affect the organization. Risk can be managed in a number of different ways, including acceptance, avoidance, transfer, or control. Internal controls are a common method for reducing the potential negative impact of risk and uncertainty.

2. The internal audit activity's audit plan should be designed based on an assessment of risk and exposures that may affect the organization. Ultimately, key audit objectives are to provide

management with information to mitigate the negative consequences associated with accomplishing the organization's objectives, as well as an assessment of the effectiveness of management's risk management activities. The degree or materiality of exposure can be viewed as risk mitigated by establishing control activities.

3. The audit universe can include components from the organization's strategic plan. By incorporating components of the organization's strategic plan, the audit universe will consider and reflect the overall business' objectives. Strategic plans also likely reflect the organization's attitude toward risk and the degree of difficulty to achieving planned objectives. The audit universe will normally be influenced by the results of the risk management process. The organization's strategic plan should have been created considering the environment in which the organization operates. These same environmental factors would likely impact the audit universe and assessment of relative risk.

4. Changes in management direction, objectives, emphasis, and focus should be reflected in updates to the audit universe and related audit plan. It is advisable to assess the audit universe on at least an annual basis to reflect the most current strategies and direction of the organization. In some situations, audit plans may need to be updated frequently (e.g., quarterly) in response to changes in the organization's environment of management activities.

5. Audit work schedules should be based on, among other factors, an assessment of risk priority and exposure. Prioritizing is needed to make decisions for applying relative resources based on the significance of risk and exposure. A variety of risk models exist to assist the chief audit executive in prioritizing potential audit subject areas. Most risk models utilize risk factors to establish the priority of engagements such as: financial impact; asset

liquidity; management competence; quality of internal controls; degree of change or stability; time of last audit engagement; complexity; employee and government relations; etc. In conducting audit engagements, methods and techniques for testing and validating exposures should be reflective of the risk materiality and likelihood of occurrence.

6. Management reporting and communication should convey risk management conclusions and recommendations to reduce exposures. For management to fully understand the degree of exposure, it is critical that audit reporting identify the criticality and consequence of the risk exposure to achieving objectives.

Practice Advisory 2020-1: Communication and Approval

Interpretation of *Standard 2020* from the *International Standards for the Professional Practice of Internal Auditing*

Related Standard

2020 – Communication and Approval

The chief audit executive should communicate the internal audit activity's plans and resource requirements, including significant interim changes, to senior management and the board for review and approval. The chief audit executive should also communicate the impact of resource limitations.

Nature of this Practice Advisory: Internal auditors should consider the following suggestions when communicating and seeking approval of the internal audit activity plans and resources. This guidance is not intended to represent all the considerations that may be necessary, but simply a recommended set of items that should be addressed.

1. The chief audit executive (CAE) should submit annually to the board for approval, and senior management as appropriate, a summary of the internal audit activity's work schedule, staffing plan, and financial budget. The CAE should also submit all significant interim changes for approval and information. Engagement work schedules, staffing plans, and financial budgets should inform senior management and the board of the scope of internal auditing work and of any limitations placed on that scope.

2. The approved engagement work schedule, staffing plan, and financial budget, along with all significant interim changes, should contain sufficient information to enable the board to ascertain whether the internal audit activity's objectives and plans support those of the organization and the board.

Practice Advisory 2030-1: Resource Management

Interpretation of *Standard 2030* from the *International Standards for the Professional Practice of Internal Auditing*

> *Related Standard*
> **2030 – Resource Management**
> The chief audit executive should ensure that internal audit resources are appropriate, sufficient, and effectively deployed to achieve the approved plan.

Nature of this Practice Advisory: Internal auditors should consider the following suggestions when evaluating internal audit resources. This guidance is not intended to represent all the considerations that may be necessary during such an evaluation, but simply a recommended set of items that should be addressed.

1. Staffing plans and financial budgets, including the number of auditors and the knowledge, skills, and other competencies required to perform their work, should be determined from engagement work schedules, administrative activities, education and training requirements, and audit research and development efforts.

2. The chief audit executive (CAE) should establish a program for selecting and developing the human resources of the internal audit activity. The program should provide for:

- Developing written job descriptions for each level of the audit staff.
- Selecting individuals who are qualified and competent regarding the areas being audited and in applying internal auditing skills.
- Training and providing continuing educational opportunities for each internal auditor.
- Establishing annual performance objectives for internal auditors.
- Appraising each internal auditor's performance at least annually.
- Providing counsel to internal auditors on their performance and professional development.

3. The CAE should consider using persons from co-sourcing arrangements, other consultants, or company employees from other departments to provide specialized or additional skills where needed.

Practice Advisory 2040-1: Policies and Procedures

Interpretation of *Standard 2040* from the *International Standards for the Professional Practice of Internal Auditing*

Related Standard
2040 – Policies and Procedures
The chief audit executive should establish policies and procedures to guide the internal audit activity.

Nature of this Practice Advisory: Internal auditors should consider the following suggestions when establishing policies and procedures. This guidance is not intended to represent all the considerations that may be necessary, but simply a recommended set of items that should be addressed.

1. The form and content of written policies and procedures should be appropriate to the size and structure of the internal audit activity and the complexity of its work. Formal administrative and technical audit manuals may not be needed by all internal auditing entities. A small internal audit activity may be managed informally. Its audit staff may be directed and controlled through daily, close supervision and written memoranda. In a large internal audit activity, more formal and comprehensive policies and procedures are essential to guide the audit staff in the consistent compliance with the internal audit activity's standards of performance.

Practice Advisory 2050-1: Coordination

Interpretation of *Standard 2050* **from the**
International Standards for the
Professional Practice of Internal Auditing

Related Standard
2050 – Coordination
The chief audit executive should share information and coordinate activities with other internal and external providers of relevant assurance and consulting services to ensure proper coverage and minimize duplication of efforts.

Nature of this Practice Advisory: Internal auditors should consider the following suggestions when coordinating activities with other providers of relevant assurance and consulting services. This guidance is not intended to represent all the considerations that may be necessary, but simply a recommended set of items that should be addressed.

1. Internal and external auditing work should be coordinated to ensure adequate audit coverage and to minimize duplicate efforts. The scope of internal auditing work encompasses a systematic, disciplined approach to evaluate and improve the effectiveness of risk management, control, and governance processes. The scope of internal auditing work is described within Section 2100 of the *International Standards for the Professional Practice of Internal Auditing (Standards)*. On the other hand, the external auditors' ordinary examination is designed to obtain sufficient evidential matter to support an opinion on the overall

fairness of the annual financial statements. The scope of the work of external auditors is determined by their professional standards, and they are responsible for judging the adequacy of procedures performed and evidence obtained for purposes of expressing their opinion on the annual financial statements.

2. Oversight of the work of external auditors, including coordination with the internal audit activity, is the responsibility of the board. Actual coordination should be the responsibility of the chief audit executive (CAE). The CAE will require the support of the board to achieve effective coordination of audit work.

3. In coordinating the work of internal auditors with the work of external auditors, the CAE should ensure that work to be performed by internal auditors in fulfillment of Section 2100 of the *Standards* does not duplicate the work of external auditors, which can be relied on for purposes of internal auditing coverage. To the extent that professional and organizational reporting responsibilities allow, internal auditors should conduct engagements in a manner that allows for maximum audit coordination and efficiency.

4. The CAE may agree to perform work for external auditors in connection with their annual audit of the financial statements. Work performed by internal auditors to assist external auditors in fulfilling their responsibility is subject to all relevant provisions of the *Standards*.

5. The CAE should make regular evaluations of the coordination between internal and external auditors. Such evaluations may also include assessments of the overall efficiency and effectiveness of internal and external auditing functions, including aggregate audit cost.

6. In exercising its oversight role, the board may request the CAE to assess the performance of external auditors. Such assessments should ordinarily be made in the context of the CAE's role of coordinating internal and external auditing activities, and should extend to other performance matters only at the specific request of senior management or the board. Assessments of the performance of external auditors should be based on sufficient information to support the conclusions reached. Assessments of the external auditors' performance with respect to the coordination of internal and external auditing activities should reflect the criteria described in this Practice Advisory.

7. Assessments of the performance of external auditors extending to matters beyond coordination with the internal auditors may address additional factors, such as:
   • Professional knowledge and experience.
   • Knowledge of the organization's industry.
   • Independence.
   • Availability of specialized services.
   • Anticipation of and responsiveness to the needs of the organization.
   • Reasonable continuity of key engagement personnel.
   • Maintenance of appropriate working relationships.
   • Achievement of contract commitments.
   • Delivery of overall value to the organization.

8. The CAE should communicate the results of evaluations of coordination between internal and external auditors to senior management and the board along with, as appropriate, any relevant comments about the performance of external auditors.

9. External auditors may be required by their professional standards to ensure that certain matters are communicated to the board. The CAE should communicate with external auditors regarding

these matters so as to have an understanding of the issues. These matters may include:

- Issues that may affect the independence of the external auditors.
- Significant control weaknesses.
- Errors and irregularities.
- Illegal acts.
- Management judgments and accounting estimates.
- Significant audit adjustments.
- Disagreements with management.
- Difficulties encountered in performing the audit.

10. Coordination of audit efforts involves periodic meetings to discuss matters of mutual interest:

- **Audit coverage.** Planned audit activities of internal and external auditors should be discussed to assure that audit coverage is coordinated and duplicate efforts are minimized. Sufficient meetings should be scheduled during the audit process to assure coordination of audit work and efficient and timely completion of audit activities, and to determine whether observations and recommendations from work performed to date require that the scope of planned work be adjusted.
- **Access to each other's audit programs and working papers.** Access to the external auditors' programs and working papers may be important in order for internal auditors to be satisfied as to the acceptability for internal audit purposes of relying on the external auditors' work. Such access carries with it the responsibility for internal auditors to respect the confidentiality of those programs and working papers. Similarly, access to the internal auditors' programs and working papers should be given to external auditors in order for external auditors to be satisfied as to the acceptability, for external audit purposes, of relying on the internal auditors' work.

- **Exchange of audit reports and management letters.**
Internal audit final communications, management's responses
to those communications, and subsequent internal audit
activity follow-up reviews should be made available to
external auditors. These communications assist external
auditors in determining and adjusting the scope of work. In
addition, the internal auditors need access to the external
auditors' management letters. Matters discussed in
management letters assist internal auditors in planning the
areas to emphasize in future internal audit work. After review
of management letters and initiation of any needed corrective
action by appropriate members of management and the
board, the CAE should ensure that appropriate follow-up
and corrective action have been taken.
- **Common understanding of audit techniques, methods,
and terminology.** First, the CAE should understand the
scope of work planned by external auditors and should be
satisfied that the external auditors' planned work, in
conjunction with the internal auditors' planned work, satisfies
the requirements of Section 2100 of the *Standards*. Such
satisfaction requires an understanding of the level of
materiality used by external auditors for planning and the
nature and extent of the external auditors' planned
procedures.

Second, the CAE should ensure that the external auditors'
techniques, methods, and terminology are sufficiently
understood by internal auditors to enable the CAE to (1)
coordinate internal and external auditing work; (2) evaluate,
for purposes of reliance, the external auditors' work; and
(3) ensure that internal auditors who are to perform work to
fulfill the external auditors' objectives can communicate
effectively with external auditors.

Finally, the CAE should provide sufficient information to
enable external auditors to understand the internal auditors'
techniques, methods, and terminology to facilitate reliance

by external auditors on work performed using such techniques, methods, and terminology. It may be more efficient for internal and external auditors to use similar techniques, methods, and terminology to effectively coordinate their work and to rely on the work of one another.

Practice Advisory 2050-2: Acquisition of External Audit Services

Interpretation of *Standard 2050* from the *International Standards for the Professional Practice of Internal Auditing*

> ***Related Standard***
> **2050 – Coordination**
> The chief audit executive should share information and coordinate activities with other internal and external providers of relevant assurance and consulting services to ensure proper coverage and minimize duplication of efforts.

Nature of this Practice Advisory: The following guidance should be considered by chief audit executives (CAEs) when requested or assigned responsibility for acquisition of external audit services. This guidance may also be useful to the audit committee and to financial management if they are charged with obtaining external audit services. The considerations contained in this Practice Advisory are not intended to represent a complete listing of all considerations that may be necessary in every situation. CAEs should adapt and adjust this guidance as necessary to fit the specific circumstances under consideration. This Practice Advisory is particularly well suited for use in acquisition of external audit services for audits of the financial statements, but it may also be useful in obtaining external audit services for other types of engagements. See PA 2050-1, "Coordination," for guidance related to "coordinating" internal and external audit activities.

1. The internal auditor's participation in the selection, evaluation, or retention of the organization's external auditors may vary from no role in the process, to advising management or the audit committee, assistance or participation in the process, management of the process, or auditing the process. Since the *International Standards for the Professional Practice of Internal Auditing (Standards)* require internal auditors to "share information and coordinate activities with other internal and external providers of relevant assurance and consulting services," it is advisable for internal auditors to have some role or involvement in the selection or retention of the external auditors and in the definition of scope of work.

2. A board or audit committee approved policy can facilitate the periodic request for external audit services and position such exercises as normal business activities so that the present service providers do not view a decision to request proposals as a signal that the organization is dissatisfied with present services. If a specific policy does not exist, the internal auditor should determine if such services are subject to any other existing procurement policies of the organization. In the absence of appropriate policies, the internal auditor should consider facilitating development of appropriate policies.

3. Appropriate policies for selection or retention of external audit services should consider addressing the following attributes:
    *   Board or audit committee approval of the policy
    *   Nature and type of services covered by the policy
    *   Duration of contract, frequency of the formal request for services and/or determination to retain the existing service providers
    *   Participants or members of the selection and evaluation team
    *   Any critical or primary criteria that should be considered in the evaluation

- Limitations on service fees and procedures for approving exceptions to the policy
- Regulatory or other governing requirements unique to specific industries or countries

4. A board policy may also address the acquisition of services other than just financial statement audits that may be offered by external audit firms. Those may include:
   - Tax services;
   - Consulting and other non-audit services;
   - Internal audit outsourcing and/or co-sourcing services;
   - Other outsourced or co-sourced services;
   - Special services, such as agreed-upon service engagements;
   - Valuation, appraisal, and actuarial services;
   - Temporary services such as recruiting, bookkeeping, technology services; and
   - Legal services provided by external audit firms.

5. Appropriate documentation should be retained concerning a periodic, formal decision to retain the existing service providers and forego or delay requests to other potential service providers.

6. A plan should be developed for the selection process that identifies the selection committee participants, key deliverables and target dates for each phase of the process, candidates from whom to request proposals, nature and extent of services to be requested, and how information will be communicated to potential candidates. Often, at the start of the selection process, an organization may conduct a comprehensive meeting with all potential candidates in which management makes a formal presentation to cover pertinent information for the service request and supplies the candidates with a formal information package or report describing the services being requested. This general meeting can be followed with individual, on-site meetings for each candidate and include appropriate management

representatives. Other combinations of meetings and information packages are also practical or appropriate for special situations.

7. A two-phased request may be necessary to facilitate a screening process to narrow or reduce the field of potential service providers to a reasonable number of final candidates. Initial information requests should be focused on obtaining appropriate statements of qualifications, including background and other general information about the potential candidates. Information should be obtained, such as history of the firm, size of the firm, resources available, firm philosophy and audit approach, special expertise, local or servicing office that would handle the engagement, related industry experience, and biographies of key team members that would be assigned to the engagement.

8. After the initial screening process, those candidates selected to advance to the next phase should be sent a second request for information that provides more specifics about the services requested. A detailed service request that itemizes deliverables expected and key target dates should be developed. Candidates should be requested to provide specific details, including pricing for the services. A timetable for the remainder of the process can be supplied that schedules dates for delivery of the additional information requested, meetings for presentations by the candidates to the selection committee, and a date for the final selection. The detailed service request should be specific for each of the services requested and should indicate whether the services may be awarded as one package or split between multiple candidates.

9. It may be appropriate to compare and summarize the attributes of the candidates by key criteria and provide it in a format that facilitates consistent evaluation of all the service providers. Questions may be supplied that stimulate thought processes and focus the evaluation on key criteria. An evaluation form can

facilitate collection of each participant's analysis and conclusions about each of the candidates. Background information, such as the organization's past history with the various candidates, type of services previously provided, and fee history, can provide the selection team with an appropriate perspective to begin the evaluation.

10. Service arrangements for external audit engagements should be documented in a written agreement and signed by both the service provider and the engagement client.

11. If the selection process results in a change in the service providers, appropriate transition plans should be developed to facilitate a smooth and orderly change. Notifications to appropriate parties, including regulatory bodies, if required, should be communicated in a timely manner.

12. Internal auditors should determine how the organization monitors ongoing service activities from external auditors. Compliance with the terms of service contracts and other agreements should be assessed on a periodic basis. Assessment of the independence of the external auditors should include internal audit participation, be performed at least annually, and be communicated to the audit committee.

Practice Advisory 2060-1: Reporting to Board and Senior Management

Interpretation of *Standard 2060* from the *International Standards for the Professional Practice of Internal Auditing*

Related Standard
2060 – Reporting to Board and Senior Management
The chief audit executive should report periodically to the board and senior management on the internal audit activity's purpose, authority, responsibility, and performance relative to its plan. Reporting should also include significant risk exposures and control issues, corporate governance issues, and other matters needed or requested by the board and senior management.

Nature of this Practice Advisory: Internal auditors should consider the following suggestions when reporting to the board and senior management. This guidance is not intended to represent all the considerations that may be necessary, but simply a recommended set of items that should be addressed.

1. The chief audit executive (CAE) should submit activity reports to senior management and to the board periodically throughout the year. Activity reports should highlight significant engagement observations and recommendations and should inform senior management and the board of any significant deviations from approved engagement work schedules, staffing plans, and financial budgets, and the reasons for them.

2. Significant engagement observations are those conditions that, in the judgment of the CAE, could adversely affect the organization. Significant engagement observations may include conditions dealing with irregularities, illegal acts, errors, inefficiency, waste, ineffectiveness, conflicts of interest, and control weaknesses. After reviewing such conditions with senior management, the CAE should communicate significant engagement observations and recommendations to the board, whether or not they have been satisfactorily resolved.

3. Management's responsibility is to make decisions on the appropriate action to be taken regarding significant engagement observations and recommendations. Senior management may decide to assume the risk of not correcting the reported condition because of cost or other considerations. The board should be informed of senior management's decisions on all significant observations and recommendations.

4. The CAE should consider whether it is appropriate to inform the board regarding previously reported, significant observations and recommendations in those instances when senior management and the board assumed the risk of not correcting the reported condition. This may be particularly necessary when there have been organization, board, senior management, or other changes.

5. In addition to subjects covered above, activity reports should also compare (a) actual performance with the internal audit activity's goals and audit work schedules, and (b) expenditures with financial budgets. Reports should explain the reason for major variances and indicate any action taken or needed.

Practice Advisory 2060-2:
Relationship with the Audit Committee

**Interpretation of *Standard 2060* from the
*International Standards for the
Professional Practice of Internal Auditing***

Related Standard
2060 – Reporting to Board and Senior Management
The chief audit executive should report periodically to the board
and senior management on the internal audit activity's purpose,
authority, responsibility, and performance relative to its plan.
Reporting should also include significant risk exposures and
control issues, corporate governance issues, and other matters
needed or requested by the board and senior management.

---

*Nature of this Practice Advisory: Internal auditors should
consider the following suggestions regarding the relationship
between the internal audit activity and the audit committee of
the governing body. This guidance is not intended to represent
all necessary considerations, but merely summarizes key
information concerning appropriate relationships between audit
committees and internal auditing.*

1. The term "audit committee," as used in this document, refers to
    the governance body that is charged with oversight of the
    organization's audit and control functions. Although these
    fiduciary duties are often delegated to an audit committee of the
    board of directors, the information in this Practice Advisory is
    also intended to apply to other oversight groups with equivalent
    authority and responsibility, such as trustees, legislative bodies,

owners of an owner-managed entity, internal control committees, or full boards of directors.

2. The Institute of Internal Auditors (IIA) recognizes that audit committees and internal auditors have interlocking goals. A strong working relationship with the audit committee is essential for each to fulfill its responsibilities to senior management, board of directors, shareholders, and other outside parties. This Practice Advisory summarizes The IIA's views concerning the aspects and attributes of an appropriate relationship between an audit committee and the internal audit function. The IIA acknowledges that audit committee responsibilities encompass activities that are beyond the scope of this advisory, and in no way intends it to be a comprehensive description of audit committee responsibilities.

3. There are three areas of activities that are key to an effective relationship between the audit committee and the internal audit function, chiefly through the chief audit executive (CAE):
    *   Assisting the audit committee to ensure that its charter, activities, and processes are appropriate to fulfill its responsibilities.
    *   Ensuring that the charter, role, and activities of internal audit are clearly understood and responsive to the needs of the audit committee and the board.
    *   Maintaining open and effective communications with the audit committee and the chairperson.

Audit Committee Responsibilities

4. The CAE should assist the committee in ensuring that the charter, role, and activities of the committee are appropriate for it to achieve its responsibilities. The CAE can play an important role by assisting the committee to periodically review its activities and suggesting enhancements. In this way, the CAE serves as

a valued advisor to the committee on audit committee and regulatory practices. Examples of activities that the CAE can undertake are:

- Review the charter for the audit committee at least annually and advise the committee whether the charter addresses all responsibilities directed to the committee in any terms of reference or mandates from the board of directors.
- Review or maintain a planning agenda for the audit committee's meeting that details all required activities to ascertain whether they are completed and that assists the committee in reporting to the board annually that it has completed all assigned duties.
- Draft the audit committee's meeting agenda for the chairman's review, facilitate the distribution of the material to the audit committee members, and write up the minutes of the audit committee meetings.
- Encourage the audit committee to conduct periodic reviews of its activities and practices compared with current best practices to ensure that its activities are consistent with leading practices.
- Meet periodically with the chairperson to discuss whether the materials and information being furnished to the committee are meeting their needs.
- Inquire from the audit committee if any educational or informational sessions or presentations would be helpful, such as training new committee members on risk and controls.
- Inquire from the committee whether the frequency and time allotted to the committee are sufficient.

Internal Audit Activity's Role

5. The CAE's relationship to the audit committee should revolve around a core role of the CAE ensuring that the audit committee understands, supports, and receives all assistance needed from the internal audit function. The IIA supports the concept that

sound governance is dependent on the synergy generated among the four principal components of effective corporate governance systems: boards of directors, management, internal auditors, and external auditors. In that structure, internal auditors and audit committees are mutually supportive. Consideration of the work of internal auditors is essential for the audit committee to gain a complete understanding of an organization's operations. A primary component of the CAE's role with the committee is to ensure this objective is accomplished and the committee views the CAE as their trusted advisor. The CAE can perform a number of activities to accomplish this role:

- Request that the committee review and approve the internal audit charter on an annual basis. (A model internal audit department charter is available on The IIA's Web site at http://www.theiia.org/ecm/guide-ia.cfm?doc_id=383)
- Review with the audit committee the functional and administrative reporting lines of internal audit to ensure that the organizational structure in place allows adequate independence for internal auditors. (Practice Advisory 1110-2, "Chief Audit Executive (CAE) Reporting Lines")
- Incorporate in the charter for the audit committee to review hiring decisions of the CAE, including appointment, compensation, evaluation, retention, and dismissal.
- Incorporate in the charter for the audit committee to review and approve proposals to outsource any internal audit activities.
- Assist the audit committee in evaluating the adequacy of the personnel and budget, and the scope and results of the internal audit activities, to ensure that there are no budgetary or scope limitations that impede the ability of the internal audit function to execute its responsibilities.
- Provide information on the coordination with and oversight of other control and monitoring functions (e.g., risk management, compliance, security, business continuity, legal, ethics, environmental, external audit).

- Report significant issues related to the processes for controlling the activities of the organization and its affiliates, including potential improvements to those processes, and provide information concerning such issues through resolution.
- Provide information on the status and results of the annual audit plan and the sufficiency of department resources to senior management and the audit committee.
- Develop a flexible annual audit plan using an appropriate risk-based methodology, including any risks or control concerns identified by management, and submit that plan to the audit committee for review and approval as well as periodic updates.
- Report on the implementation of the annual audit plan, as approved, including as appropriate any special tasks or projects requested by management and the audit committee.
- Incorporate into the internal audit charter the responsibility for the internal audit department to report to the audit committee on a timely basis any suspected fraud involving management or employees who are significantly involved in the internal controls of the company. Assist in the investigation of significant suspected fraudulent activities within the organization and notify management and the audit committee of the results.
- Audit committees should be made aware that quality assessment reviews of the internal audit activity be done every five years in order for the audit activity to declare that it meets The IIA's *International Standards for the Professional Practice of Internal Auditing (Standards)*. Regular quality assessment reviews will provide assurance to the audit committee and to management that internal auditing activities conform to the *Standards*.

Communications with the Audit Committee

6. While not to diminish any of the activities noted above, in a large part the overall effectiveness of the CAE and audit committee relationship will revolve around the communications between the parties. Today's audit committees expect a high level of open and candid communications. If the CAE is to be viewed as a trusted advisor by the committee, communications is the key element. Internal auditing, by definition, can help the audit committee accomplish its objectives by bringing a systematic, disciplined approach to its activities, but unless there is appropriate communications, it is not possible for the committee to determine this. The CAE should consider providing communications to the audit committee in the following areas.

    - Audit committees should meet privately with the CAE on a regular basis to discuss sensitive issues.
    - Provide an annual summary report or assessment on the results of the audit activities relating to the defined mission and scope of audit work.
    - Issue periodic reports to the audit committee and management summarizing results of audit activities.
    - Keep the audit committee informed of emerging trends and successful practices in internal auditing.
    - Together with external auditors, discuss fulfillment of committee information needs.
    - Review information submitted to the audit committee for completeness and accuracy.
    - Confirm there is effective and efficient work coordination of activities between internal and external auditors. Determine if there is any duplication between the work of the internal and external auditors and give the reasons for such duplication.

Practice Advisory 2100-1: Nature of Work

Interpretation of *Standard 2100* from the *International Standards for the Professional Practice of Internal Auditing*

Related Standard
2100 – Nature of Work
The internal audit activity should evaluate and contribute to the improvement of risk management, control, and governance processes using a systematic and disciplined approach.

Nature of this Practice Advisory: Internal auditors should consider the following suggestions when evaluating the nature of the internal audit activity's work. This guidance is not intended to represent all the considerations that may be necessary during such an evaluation, but simply a recommended set of items that should be addressed.

1. The scope of internal auditing work encompasses a systematic, disciplined approach to evaluating and improving the *adequacy* and *effectiveness* of risk management, control, and governance processes and the quality of performance in carrying out assigned responsibilities. The purposes of evaluating the adequacy of the organization's existing risk management, control, and governance processes is to provide: (1) reasonable assurance that these processes are functioning as intended and will enable the organization's objectives and goals to be met, and (2) recommendations for improving the organization's operations, in terms of both efficient and effective performance. Senior

management and the board might also provide general direction as to the scope of work and the activities to be audited.

2. *Adequacy* of risk management, control, and governance processes is present if management has planned and designed them in a manner that provides reasonable assurance that the organization's objectives and goals will be achieved efficiently and economically. Efficient performance accomplishes objectives and goals in an accurate, timely, and economical fashion. Economical performance accomplishes objectives and goals with minimal use of resources (i.e., cost) commensurate with the risk exposure. Reasonable assurance is provided if the most cost-effective measures are taken in the design and implementation stages to reduce risks and restrict expected deviations to a tolerable level. Thus, the design process begins with the establishment of objectives and goals. This is followed by connecting or interrelating concepts, parts, activities, and people in such a manner as to operate together to achieve the established objectives and goals.

3. *Effectiveness* of risk management, control, and governance processes is present if management directs processes in such a manner as to provide reasonable assurance that the organization's objectives and goals will be achieved. In addition to accomplishing the objectives and planned activities, management directs by authorizing activities and transactions, monitoring resulting performance, and verifying that the organization's processes are operating as designed.

4. Broadly, management is responsible for the sustainability of the whole organization and accountability for the organization's actions, conduct, and performance to the owners, other stakeholders, regulators, and general public. Specifically, the primary objectives of the overall management process are to achieve:

- Relevant, reliable, and credible financial and operating information.
- Effective and efficient use of the organization's resources.
- Safeguarding of the organization's assets.
- Compliance with laws, regulations, ethical and business norms, and contracts.
- Identification of risk exposures and use of effective strategies to control them.
- Established objectives and goals for operations or programs

5. Management plans, organizes, and directs the performance of sufficient actions to provide reasonable assurance that objectives and goals will be achieved. Management periodically reviews its objectives and goals and modifies its processes to accommodate changes in internal and external conditions. Management also establishes and maintains an organizational culture, including an ethical climate that understands risk exposures and implements effective risk strategies for managing them.

6. *Control* is any action taken by management to enhance the likelihood that established objectives and goals will be achieved. Controls may be preventive (to deter undesirable events from occurring), detective (to detect and correct undesirable events which have occurred), or directive (to cause or encourage a desirable event to occur). The concept of a system of control is the integrated collection of control components and activities that are used by an organization to achieve its objectives and goals.

7. Internal auditors evaluate the whole management process of planning, organizing, and directing to determine whether reasonable assurance exists that objectives and goals will be achieved. Internal auditors should be alert to actual or potential changes in internal or external conditions that affect the ability

to provide assurance from a forward-looking perspective. In those cases, internal auditors should address the risk that performance may deteriorate.

8. These internal auditing evaluations, in the aggregate, provide information to appraise the overall management process. All business systems, processes, operations, functions, and activities within the organization are subject to the internal auditors' evaluations. The comprehensive scope of work of internal auditing should provide reasonable assurance that management's:

- Risk management system is effective.
- System of internal control is adequate, effective and efficient.
- Governance process is effective by establishing and preserving values, setting goals, monitoring activities and performance, and defining the measures of accountability.

Practice Advisory 2100-2: Information Security

Interpretation of *Standard 2100* from the *International Standards for the Professional Practice of Internal Auditing*

Related Standard
2100 – Nature of Work
The internal audit activity should evaluate and contribute to the improvement of risk management, control, and governance processes using a systematic and disciplined approach.

Nature of this Practice Advisory: Internal auditors should consider the following suggestions when evaluating an organization's governance activities related to information security. This guidance is not intended to represent all the procedures necessary for a comprehensive assurance or consulting engagement related to information security, but simply a recommended core set of high level auditor responsibilities to complement related board and management responsibilities.

1. Internal auditors should determine that management and the board have a clear understanding that information security is a management responsibility. This responsibility includes all critical information of the organization regardless of media in which the information is stored.

2. The chief audit executive should determine that the internal audit activity possesses, or has access to, competent auditing resources to evaluate information security and associated risk exposures. This includes both internal and external risk exposures, including

exposures relating to the organization's relationships with outside entities.

3. Internal auditors should determine that the board has sought assurance from management that information security breaches and conditions that might represent a threat to the organization will promptly be made known to those performing the internal audit activity.

4. Internal auditors should assess the effectiveness of preventive, detective, and mitigation measures against past attacks, as deemed appropriate, and future attempts or incidents deemed likely to occur. Internal auditors should confirm that the board has been appropriately informed of threats, incidents, vulnerabilities exploited, and corrective measures.

5. Internal auditors should periodically assess the organization's information security practices and recommend, as appropriate, enhancements to, or implementation of, new controls and safeguards. Following an assessment, an assurance report should be provided to the board. Such assessments can either be conducted as separate stand-alone engagements or as multiple engagements integrated into other audits or engagements conducted as part of the approved audit plan.

Practice Advisory 2100-3:
Internal Auditing's Role in the
Risk Management Process

**Interpretation of *Standard 2100* from the
*International Standards for the
Professional Practice of Internal Auditing***

> *Related Standard*
> **2100 – Nature of Work**
> The internal audit activity should evaluate and contribute to the improvement of risk management, control, and governance processes using a systematic and disciplined approach

*Nature of this Practice Advisory: The definition of internal auditing calls for "...a disciplined approach to evaluate and improve the effectiveness of **risk management**, control, and governance processes." Internal auditors have a key role to play in an organization's risk management process in order to practice internal auditing in accordance with the Standards. This advisory seeks to provide internal auditors with guidance for determining their role in an organization's risk management process and for complying with the Standards. Additional considerations beyond those contained in this advisory may be necessary.*

1. Risk management is a key responsibility of management. To achieve its business objectives, management should ensure that sound risk management processes are in place and functioning. Boards and audit committees have an oversight role to determine that appropriate risk management processes are in place and

that these processes are adequate and effective. Internal auditors should assist both management and the audit committee by examining, evaluating, reporting, and recommending improvements on the adequacy and effectiveness of management's risk processes. Management and the board are responsible for their organization's risk management and control processes. However, internal auditors acting in a consulting role can assist the organization in identifying, evaluating, and implementing risk management methodologies and controls to address those risks.

2. Developing assessments and reports on the organization's risk management processes are normally a high audit priority. Evaluating management's risk processes is different than the requirement that auditors use risk analysis to plan audits. However, information from a comprehensive risk management process, including the identification of management and board concerns, can assist the internal auditor in planning audit activities.

3. The chief audit executive should obtain an understanding of management's and the board's expectations of the internal audit activity in the organization's risk management process. This understanding should be codified in the charters of the internal audit activity and audit committee.

4. Responsibilities and activities should be coordinated between all groups and individuals with a role in the organization's risk management process. These responsibilities and activities should be appropriately documented in the organization's strategic plans, board policies, management directives, operating procedures, and other governance type instruments. Examples of some of the activities and responsibilities that should be documented include:
   - Setting strategic direction may reside with the board or a committee;

- Ownership of risks may be assigned at the senior management level;
- Acceptance of residual risk may reside at the executive management level;
- Identifying, assessing, mitigating, and monitoring activities on a continuous basis may be assigned at the operating level; and
- Periodic assessment and assurance to others should reside with the internal audit activity.

5. Internal auditors are expected to identify and evaluate significant risk exposures in the normal course of their duties.

6. The internal audit activity's role in the risk management process of an organization can change over time and may be found at some point along a continuum that ranges from:
   - No role, to
   - Auditing the risk management process as part of the internal audit plan, to
   - Active, continuous support and involvement in the risk management process such as participation on oversight committees, monitoring activities, and status reporting, to
   - Managing and coordinating the risk management process.

7. Ultimately, it is the role of executive management and the audit committee to determine the role of internal audit in the risk management process. Management's view on internal audit's role is likely to be determined by factors such as the culture of the organization, ability of the internal auditing staff, and local conditions and customs of the country.

8. Additional guidance can be found in the following Practice Advisories:
   - PA 2100-4, "Internal Auditing's Role in Organizations Without a Risk Management Process"

- PA 1130.A1-2, "Internal Auditing's Responsibility for Other (Non-audit) Functions"
- PA 2110-1, "Assessing the Adequacy of Risk Management Processes"
- PA 2010-2, "Linking the Audit Plan to Risk and Exposure"

Practice Advisory 2100-4:
Internal Auditing's Role in Organizations
Without a Risk Management Process

Interpretation of *Standard 2100* **from the**
International Standards for the
Professional Practice of Internal Auditing

Related Standard
2100 – Nature of Work
The internal audit activity should evaluate and contribute to the improvement of risk management, control, and governance processes using a systematic and disciplined approach.

---

*Nature of this Practice Advisory: The definition of internal auditing calls for "...a disciplined approach to evaluate and improve the effectiveness of **risk management**, control, and governance processes." Internal auditors have a key role to play in an organization's risk management process in order to practice internal auditing in accordance with the Standards. However, some organizations may not have an established risk management process. This advisory seeks to provide internal auditors with guidance for determining their role in an organization without an established risk management process. Additional considerations beyond those contained in this advisory may be necessary.*

1. Risk management is a key responsibility of management. To achieve its business objectives, management should ensure that sound risk management processes are in place and functioning. Boards and audit committees have an oversight role to determine

that appropriate risk management processes are in place and that these processes are adequate and effective. Internal auditors should assist both management and the audit committee by examining, evaluating, reporting, and recommending improvements on the adequacy and effectiveness of management's risk processes. Management and the board are responsible for their organization's risk management and control processes. However, internal auditors acting in a consulting role can assist the organization in identifying, evaluating, and implementing risk management methodologies and controls to address those risks.

2. Developing assessments and reports on the organization's risk management processes are normally a high audit priority. Evaluating management's risk processes is different than the requirement that auditors use risk analysis to plan audits. However, information from a comprehensive risk management process, including the identification of management and board concerns, can assist the internal auditor in planning audit activities.

3. The chief audit executive should obtain an understanding of management's and the board's expectations of the internal audit activity in the organization's risk management process. This understanding should be codified in the charters of the internal audit activity and audit committee.

4. If an organization has not established a risk management process, the internal auditor should bring this to management's attention along with suggestions for establishing such a process. The internal auditor should seek direction from management and the board as to the audit activity's role in the risk management process. The charters for the audit activity and audit committee should document the role of each in the risk management process.

5. If requested, internal auditors can play a proactive role in assisting with the initial establishment of a risk management process for the organization. A more proactive role supplements traditional assurance activities with a consultative approach to improving fundamental processes. If such assistance exceeds normal assurance and consulting activities conducted by internal auditors, independence could be impaired. In these situations, internal auditors should comply with the disclosure requirements of the *International Standards for the Professional Practice of Internal Auditing (Standards)*. Additional guidance can also be found in Practice Advisory 1130.A1-2, "Internal Auditing's Responsibility for Other (Non-audit) Functions."

6. A proactive role in developing and managing a risk management process is not the same as an "ownership of risks" role. In order to avoid an "ownership of risk" role, internal auditors should seek confirmation from management as to its responsibility for identification, mitigation, monitoring, and "ownership" of risks.

7. In summary, internal auditors can facilitate or enable risk management processes, but they should not "own" or be responsible for the management of the risks identified.

Practice Advisory 2100-5:
Legal Considerations in Evaluating
Regulatory Compliance Programs

*Interpretation of Standard 2100 from the
International Standards for the
Professional Practice of Internal Auditing*

**Related Standard
2100 – Nature of Work**
The internal audit activity should evaluate and contribute to the improvement of risk management, control, and governance processes using a systematic and disciplined approach.

Nature of this Practice Advisory: Internal auditors should consider the following suggestions when evaluating an organization's regulatory compliance programs. This guidance is not intended to represent all the procedures that may be necessary for a comprehensive assurance or consulting engagement related to regulatory compliance.

Caution – *Internal auditors are encouraged to consult legal counsel in all matters involving legal issues as requirements may vary significantly in different jurisdictions. The guidance contained in this Practice Advisory is based primarily on the United States' legal system.*

1. Compliance programs assist organizations in preventing inadvertent employee violations, detecting illegal activities, and discouraging intentional employee violations. They can also help prove insurance claims, determine director and officer liability,

create or enhance corporate identity, and decide the appropriateness of punitive damages. Internal auditors should evaluate an organization's regulatory compliance programs in light of the following suggested steps for effective compliance programs.

2. The organization should establish compliance standards and procedures to be followed by its employees and other agents that are reasonably capable of reducing the prospect of criminal conduct.

    - The organization should develop a written business code of conduct that clearly identifies prohibited activities. This code should be written in language that all employees can understand, avoiding legalese.

    - A good code provides guidance to employees on relevant issues. Checklists, a question and answer section, and reference to additional sources for further information all help make the code user friendly.

    - The organization should create an organizational chart identifying board members, senior officers, senior compliance officer, and department personnel who are responsible for implementing compliance programs.

    - Codes of conduct that are viewed as legalistic and "one-sided" by employees may increase the risk that employees will engage in unethical or illegal behavior, whereas codes that are viewed as straightforward and fair tend to decrease the risk that employees will engage in such activity.

    - Companies using reward systems that attach financial incentives to apparently unethical or illegal behavior can expect a poor compliance environment.

    - Companies with international operations should institute a compliance program on a global basis, not just for selective geographic locations. Such programs should reflect appropriate local conditions, laws, and regulations.

3. Specific individual(s) within high-level personnel of the organization should be assigned overall responsibility to oversee regulatory compliance with standards and procedures.

    - High-level personnel of the organization means individuals who have substantial control of the organization or who have a substantial role in the making of policy within the organization.

    - High-level personnel of the organization includes: a director; an executive officer; an individual in charge of a major business or functional unit of the organization, such as sales, administration or finance; and an individual with a substantial ownership interest.

    - To be fully effective, the CEO and other senior management must have significant involvement in the program.

    - In some organizations assigning chief compliance responsibilities to the company's general counsel may convince employees that management is not committed to the program, and that the program is important to the legal department only, not the firm as a whole. In other organizations the opposite may be true.

    - In a large company with several business units, compliance responsibilities should be assigned to high-level personnel in each unit.

    - It is not enough for the company to create the position of chief compliance officer and to select the rest of the compliance unit. The company should also ensure that those personnel are appropriately empowered and supplied with the resources necessary for carrying out their mission. Compliance personnel should have adequate access to senior management. The chief compliance officer should report directly to the CEO.

4. The organization should use due care not to delegate substantial discretionary authority to individuals whom the organization

knows, or should know through the exercise of due diligence, has a propensity to engage in illegal activities.

- Companies should screen applicants for employment at all levels for evidence of past wrongdoing, especially wrongdoing within the company's industry.
- Employment applications should inquire as to past criminal convictions. Professionals should be asked about any history of discipline in front of licensing boards.
- Care should be taken to ensure that the company does not infringe upon employees' and applicants' privacy rights under applicable laws. Many jurisdictions have laws limiting the amount of information a company can obtain in performing background checks on employees.

5. The organization should take steps to communicate effectively its standards and procedures to all employees and other agents, e.g., by requiring participation in training programs or by disseminating publications that explain in a practical manner what is required.

- The effectiveness of a compliance program will depend upon the ways in which it is communicated to employees. Generally, an interactive format works better than a lecture. Programs communicated in person tend to work better than programs communicated entirely through video or game formats. Programs that are periodically repeated work better than onetime presentations.
- The best programs include employee training that allows employees to practice new techniques and use new information. Such activities are particularly appropriate with regard to management training, but are effective with regard to employees at all levels.
- The language used by an organization's code of conduct and employee manual should be easy to understand. Alternative methods of communicating the code and the employee manual to employees lacking more formal education must be found and implemented.

- Compliance tips, statements, and warnings should be disseminated to employees through a variety of available media: newsletters, posters, e-mail, questionnaires, and presentations.
- Organizations should present the program on multiple occasions to different sets of employees, targeting the information presented to the areas important to each functional group of employees. The information should be tailored to that group's job requirements. For example, environmental compliance information should be directed to those departments such as manufacturing or real property management that have an increased likelihood of violating or detecting violations of such laws and regulations. On the other hand, providing such training to a department with no such responsibilities could be detrimental, inspiring employee apathy or a belief that the program was not well constructed.
- New employees should receive basic compliance training as part of their orientation. Later, they can be incorporated into ongoing compliance efforts in their departments.
- Agents of the organization should be asked to attend a presentation specifically geared toward them. It is important that an organization inform its agents of the organization's core values, and that the actions of its agents that are attributable to the company will be monitored in connection with the compliance program. The organization should be prepared to cease doing business with agents who fail to adhere to the organization's compliance standards.
- Organizations should require employees to periodically certify that they have read, understood, and complied with the company's code of conduct. This information should be related annually to senior management and the board of directors.
- All ethics-related documents — codes of conduct, human resources policies/manuals, etc. — should be readily available to all employees. Continuous access availability,

such as through the organization's intranet, is strongly encouraged.

6. The organization should take reasonable steps to achieve compliance with its standards, e.g., by utilizing monitoring and auditing systems reasonably designed to detect criminal conduct by its employees and other agents and by having in place and publicizing a reporting system whereby employees and other agents could report criminal conduct by others within the organization without fear of retribution.

    - The organization should devote an amount of resources to the internal audit plan that is appropriate given the size of the company and the difficulty of the audit task. The audit plan should concentrate on the organization's activities in each of its businesses.

    - The audit plan should also include a review of the organization's compliance program and its procedures, including reviews to determine whether: written materials are effective, communications have been received by employees, detected violations have been appropriately handled, discipline has been evenhanded, whistleblowers have not been retaliated against, and the compliance unit has fulfilled its responsibilities. The auditors should review the compliance program to determine whether it can be improved, and should solicit employee input in that regard.

    - Each program should have a "hot line" or other reporting system under which employees can report activity that they believe to be unethical, illegal, or against the company's code of conduct. Employees must be free to report such behavior without fear of reprisal.

    - Although an attorney monitoring the hot line is better able to protect attorney-client and work-product privileges, one study observed that employees have little confidence in hot lines answered by the legal department or by an outside service. The same study showed that employees have even less confidence in write-in reports or an off-site ombudsperson, but have the most confidence in hot lines answered by an in-house representative and backed by a non-retaliation policy.

- Use of an on-site ombudsperson is more effective if the ombudsperson reports directly to the chief compliance officer or the board of directors, if the ombudsperson can keep the names of whistleblowers secret, if the ombudsperson provides guidance to whistleblowers, and if the ombudsperson undertakes follow-up review to ensure that retaliation has not occurred. Additionally, some jurisdictions now recognize a limited ombudsperson privilege under which the ombudsperson is protected from disclosing confidential communications made by whistleblowers to the ombudsperson.

- An effective tool for uncovering unethical or illegal activity is the ethics questionnaire. Each employee of the organization should receive a questionnaire, which asks whether the employee is aware of kickbacks, bribes, or other wrongdoing. To protect privilege, the questionnaire should be sent by organization counsel, contain a statement that the questionnaire is protected by privilege, require the employee to complete, sign, and return the questionnaire without making a copy, and contain a statement that the organization retains the right to disclose information provided to the company to government agencies or in litigation. Note that privilege will be lost if the questionnaire is disclosed to outside parties.

7. The standards should be consistently enforced through appropriate disciplinary mechanisms, including, as appropriate, discipline of individuals responsible for the failure to detect an offense. Adequate discipline of individuals responsible for an offense is a necessary component of enforcement; however, the form of discipline that will be appropriate will be case specific.

- The compliance program should contain a disciplinary system under which those who violate the organization's code of conduct receive punishment appropriate to the offense, such as warning, loss of pay, suspension, transfer, or termination. But if an employee is found to have committed some illegal act, the organization might have to terminate that employee, in keeping with the organization's obligation to use "due care not to delegate substantial discretionary authority to individuals whom the organization knew, or should have known through the exercise of due diligence, had a propensity to engage in illegal activities."

- Discipline under the program must be fair. The program has slight chance of succeeding if unethical or illegal activity goes unpunished, especially if tied to the activities of senior management or big producers. Ignored wrongdoing by such persons will encourage such behavior in the rest of the workforce.

- Termination or other discipline of employees may be limited by whistleblower laws, exceptions to the employee-at-will doctrine, employee or union contracts, and employer responsibilities with regard to discrimination, wrongful discharge, and employer bad faith laws/doctrines.

- The program should provide for the discipline of managers and other responsible persons who knew or should have known of misconduct and did not report it. Failure of the program to do so may cause a court to find that the program is not effective; the program will then have no beneficial effect on sentencing.

- Organizations should be scrupulous and thorough in documenting employee discipline. The organization should be able to prove that it made its best efforts to collect information with regard to any incident and took appropriate action based upon the information available.

8. After an offense has been detected, the organization should take
    all reasonable steps to respond appropriately to the offense and
    to prevent further similar offenses — including any necessary
    modifications to its program to prevent and detect violations of
    law.

    *   The organization should respond appropriately to each offense
        detected by the compliance program. Appropriate responses
        include disciplinary action taken with regard to those who
        engaged in misconduct.

    *   In some circumstances, an appropriate response could
        require self-reporting the violation to the government,
        cooperation with governmental investigations, and the
        acceptance of responsibility for the violation. Note that
        similar to the existence of an effective compliance program,
        making these responses could result in a court lowering the
        amount of the organization's fine.

    *   Failure to detect or prevent a serious violation could indicate
        that the compliance program needs a major overhaul. At a
        minimum, after any violation is detected compliance personnel
        should examine the program to determine whether changes
        need to be made.

    *   One change that may be required in light of a violation could
        be the replacement or shuffling of compliance personnel. In
        fact, the organization may need to discipline or replace any
        manager who fails to detect or prevent misconduct in the
        areas under the manager's supervision, especially if the
        violation is one that the manager should have detected.

Practice Advisory 2100-6:
Control and Audit Implications of
E-commerce Activities

Interpretation of *Standard 2100* from the
International Standards for the
Professional Practice of Internal Auditing

Related Standard
2100 – Nature of Work
The internal audit activity should evaluate and contribute to the improvement of risk management, control, and governance processes using a systematic and disciplined approach.

Nature of this Practice Advisory: Growth of e-commerce continues at a fast pace, both for business-to-business or business-to-consumer applications. Effective controls and processes are critical for successful development and implementation of an e-commerce strategy. Thus, an effective e-commerce assessment effort may be a key part of the annual audit plan for many companies. This PA provides an overview of the control and audit implications. Additional resources for practitioners are: IIA's Systems Assurance and Control (SAC) *product and other technology reports and ISACA's publications. Both have developed guidelines and criteria for evaluation of electronic systems and models.*

1. Electronic commerce (e-commerce) is generally defined as "conducting commercial activities over the Internet." These commercial activities can be business-to-business (B2B), business-to-consumer (B2C), and business-to-employee (B2E).

The growth of e-commerce has been dramatic and is anticipated to grow even more rapidly in the years ahead. The recent publication by The IIA Research Foundation, *Systems Assurance and Control (SAC),* and the success of the Web-based *www.ITAudit.org* and various e-mail IIA newsletters confirms that technology not only supports e-commerce strategies, but is an integral part. Web-based and other technology changes have a dramatic impact on society, governance, economics, competition, markets, organizational structure, and national defense. Clearly, these changes and the dramatic growth of e-commerce create significant control and management challenges that should be considered by internal auditors in developing and implementing their audit plans.

Understanding and Planning an E-commerce Engagement

2. Continuous changes in technology offer the internal auditing profession both great opportunity and risk. Before attempting to provide assurance on the systems and processes, an internal auditor should understand the changes in business and information systems, the related risks, and the alignment of strategies with the enterprise's design and market requirements. The internal auditor should review management's strategic planning and risk assessment processes and its decisions about:
   - Which risks are serious?
   - Which risks can be insured?
   - What current controls will mitigate the risks?
   - Which additional compensating controls are necessary?
   - What type of monitoring is required?

3. The major components of auditing e-commerce activities are:
   - Assess the internal control structure, including the tone set by senior management,
   - Provide reasonable assurance that goals and objectives can be achieved,

- Determine if the risks are acceptable,
- Understand the information flow,
- Review the interface issues (such as hardware to hardware, software to software, and hardware to software), and
- Evaluate the business continuity and disaster recovery plans.

4. The chief audit executive's (CAE's) concerns in performing an e-commerce engagement relate to the competency and capacity of the internal audit activity. Among the possible factors that may constrain the internal audit activity are:
   - Does the internal audit activity have sufficient skills? If not, can the skills be acquired?
   - Are training or other resources necessary?
   - Is the staffing level sufficient for the near-term and long-term?
   - Can the expected audit plan be delivered?

5. **Internal auditor's questions during risk assessment.** The IIA's *SAC* publication can assist the internal auditor in audit planning and risk assessment. It includes a list of e-commerce areas that should be of interest to an internal auditor who is undertaking an engagement and assessing risks. The questions for internal auditors to consider are:
   - Is there a business plan for the e-commerce project or program?
   - Does the plan cover the integration of the planning, design, and implementation of the e-commerce system with the strategies of the organization?
   - What will be the impact on the performance, security, reliability, and availability of the system?
   - Will the functionality meet the end user's needs (e.g., employees, customers, business partners) as well as management's objectives?
   - Have governmental and regulatory requirements been analyzed and considered?

- How secure is the hardware and software, and will they prevent or detect unauthorized access, inappropriate use, and other harmful effects and losses?
- Will transaction processing be current, accurate, complete, and indisputable?
- Does the control environment allow the organization to achieve its e-commerce objectives as it moves from concepts to results?
- Does the risk assessment include internal and external forces?
- Have the inherent risks associated with the Internet and Internet provider (such as reliability of basic communications, authentication of users, and who has access) been addressed?
- Have other issues been addressed (for example, disclosures of confidential business information, misuse of intellectual property, violations of copyrights, trademark infringement, libelous statements on Web sites, fraud, misuse of electronic signatures, privacy violations, and reputation damage)?
- If outside vendors are used, has a "going concern" evaluation been conducted by a trusted third party who is qualified to certify the vendor?
- If vendors provide hosting services, do they have a tested business contingency plan? Have they provided a recent SAS-70 report? (SAS 70 reports can offer valuable information about internal controls to user organizations.) Also, have privacy issues been resolved?
- Does the contract include audit rights?

E-commerce Risks and Control Issues

6. The e-commerce risk and control environment is complex and evolving. Risk can be defined as the uncertainty of an event occurring that could have a negative impact on the achievement of objectives. Risk is inherent to every business or government

entity. Opportunity risks assumed by management are often drivers of organizational activities. Beyond these opportunities may be threats and other dangers that are not clearly understood and fully evaluated and too easily accepted as part of doing business. In striving to manage risk, it is essential to have an understanding of risk elements. It is also important to be aware of new threats and changes in technology that open new vulnerabilities in information security. For management purposes, the seven key questions below can serve to identify organizational risk and target potential ways to control or mitigate the exposures. (Risk practitioners use a variety of different risk management approaches; these questions illustrate one approach.) Risk elements associated with the questions are displayed in brackets.

(a) Risk Identification and Quantification:
- What could happen that would adversely affect the organization's ability to achieve its objectives and execute its strategies? [Threat Events]
- If it happens, what is the potential financial impact? [Single Loss Exposure Value]
- How often might it happen? [Frequency]
- How probable are the answers to the first three questions? [Uncertainty]

(b) Risk Management and Mitigation:
- What can be done to prevent and avoid, mitigate, and detect risks and provide notification? [Safeguards and Controls]
- How much will it cost? [Safeguard and Control Costs]
- How efficient would that be? [Cost/Benefit or ROI Analysis]

7. Some of the more critical risk and control issues to be addressed by the internal auditor are:
- General project management risks.
- Specific security threats, such as denial of service, physical attacks, viruses, identity theft, and unauthorized access or disclosure of data.

- Maintenance of transaction integrity under a complex network of links to legacy systems and data warehouses.
- Web site content review and approval when there are frequent changes and sophisticated customer features and capabilities that offer around-the-clock service.
- Rapid technology changes.
- Legal issues, such as increasing regulations throughout the world to protect individual privacy; enforceability of contracts outside the organization's country; and tax and accounting issues.
- Changes to surrounding business processes and organizational structures.

Auditing E-commerce Activities

8. The overall audit objective should be to ensure that all e-commerce processes have effective internal controls. Management of e-commerce initiatives should be documented in a strategic plan that is well developed and approved. If there is a decision not to participate in e-commerce, that decision should be carefully analyzed, documented, and approved by the governing board.

9. Audit objectives for an e-commerce engagement may include:
   - Evidence of e-commerce transactions.
   - Availability and reliability of security system.
   - Effective interface between e-commerce and financial systems.
   - Security of monetary transactions.
   - Effectiveness of customer authentication process.
   - Adequacy of business continuity processes, including the resumption of operations.
   - Compliance with common security standards.
   - Effective use and control of digital signatures.

- Adequacy of systems, policies, and procedures to control public key certificates (using public key cryptographic techniques).
- Adequacy and timeliness of operating data and information.
- Documented evidence of an effective system of internal control.

10. The details of the audit program used to audit e-commerce activities in specific organizations will vary depending on industry, country, and legal and business models. The following is an outline of a possible e-commerce audit protocol for key areas.

   (a) **E-commerce organization** — The internal auditor should do the following:
   - Determine the value of transactions.
   - Identify the stakeholders (external and internal).
   - Review the change management process.
   - Examine the approval process.
   - Review the business plan for e-commerce activities.
   - Evaluate the policies over public key certificates.
   - Review the digital signature procedures.
   - Examine service-level agreements between buyer, supplier, and certification authority.
   - Ascertain the quality assurance policy.
   - Assess the privacy policy and compliance in e-commerce activities.
   - Assess the incident response capability.

   (b) **Fraud** — The internal auditor should be alert for the following conditions.
   - Unauthorized movement of money (e.g., transfers to jurisdictions where the recovery of funds would be difficult).
   - Duplication of payments.
   - Denial of orders placed or received, goods received, or payments made.

- Exception reports and procedures: and effectiveness of the follow-up.
- Digital signatures: Are they used for all transactions? Who authorizes them? Who has access to them?
- Protections against viruses and hacking activities (history file, use of tools).
- Access rights: Are they reviewed regularly? Are they promptly revised when staff members are changed?
- History of interception of transactions by unauthorized persons.

(c) **Authentication** — The internal auditor should review the policies for authenticating transactions and evaluating controls.

- Evidence of regular reviews.
- Control self-assessment (CSA) tools used by management.
- Regular independent checks.
- Segregation of duties.
- Tools that management should have in place: firewalls (multilevel to partition e-commerce and other activities), password management, independent reconciliation, and audit trails.

(d) **Corruption of data** – The internal auditor should evaluate controls over data integrity.

- Who can amend catalogs and prices or rates? What is the approval mechanism?
- Can someone destroy audit trails?
- Who can approve bulletin board amendments?
- What are the procedures for ordering and recording?
- Is the process of online tendering providing adequate documentation?
- Tools that should be in place include: intrusion management (monitoring software, automatic time-out, and trend analysis), physical security for e-commerce servers, change controls, and reconciliation.

(e) **Business interruptions** – The internal auditor should review the business continuity plan and determine if it has been tested. Management should have devised an alternative means to process the transactions in the event of an interruption. Management should have a process in place to address the following potential conditions:
- Volume attacks
- Denial of service attacks
- Inadequacies in interfacing between e-commerce and financial management systems
- Backup facilities
- Strategies to counter: hacking, intrusion, cracking, viruses, worms, Trojan horses, and back doors

(f) **Management issues** — The internal auditor should evaluate how well business units are managing the e-commerce process. The following are some relevant topics.
- Project management reviews of individual initiatives and development projects
- System Development Life Cycle reviews
- Vendor selection, vendor capabilities, employee confidentiality, and bonding
- Post-implementation economic reviews: Are anticipated benefits being achieved? What metrics are being used to measure success?
- Post-implementation process reviews: Are new processes in place and working effectively?

Practice Advisory 2100-7: Internal Auditing's Role in Identifying and Reporting Environmental Risks

Interpretation of *Standard 2100* from the *International Standards for the Professional Practice of Internal Auditing*

Related Standard
2100 – Nature of Work
The internal audit activity should evaluate and contribute to the improvement of risk management, control, and governance processes using a systematic and disciplined approach.

Nature of this Practice Advisory: The purpose of this Practice Advisory is to provide guidance to internal audit organizations on risk and independence issues related to environmental auditing activities. Internal auditors should be alert to the potential risks that may result from the organizational placement and reporting relationships of environmental auditors. This Practice Advisory suggests the minimum safeguards to ensure that important environmental issues are reported on a timely basis and to the appropriate level. The risks related to environmental noncompliance, fines and penalties and other mismanagement may result in significant losses for the organization.

Potential Risks

1. Chief audit executive (CAE) should include the environmental, health, and safety (EH&S) risks in any entity-wide risk

management assessment and assess the activities in a balanced manner relative to other types of risk associated with an entity's operations. Among the risk exposures that should be evaluated are: organizational reporting structures; likelihood of causing environmental harm, fines, and penalties; expenditures mandated by Environmental Protection Agency (EPA) or other governmental agencies; history of injuries and deaths; record of losses of customers, and episodes of negative publicity and loss of public image and reputation.

2. If the CAE finds that the management of the EH&S risks largely depends on an environmental audit function, the CAE needs to consider the implications of that organizational structure and its effects on operations and the reporting mechanisms. If the CAE finds that the exposures are not adequately managed and residual risks exist, that conclusion would normally result in changes to the internal audit activity's plan of engagements and further investigations.

3. The majority of environmental audit functions report to their organization's environmental component or general counsel, not to the CAE. The typical organizational models for environmental auditing fall into one of the following scenarios:
    - The CAE and environmental audit chief are in separate functional units with little contact with each other.
    - The CAE and environmental audit chief are in separate functional units and coordinate their activities.
    - The CAE has responsibility for auditing environmental issues.

4. According to an IIA flash report on environmental auditing issues:
    - About one-half of the environmental auditors seldom meet with a committee of the governing board and only 40 percent have some contact with the CAE.
    - Seventy percent of the organizations reported that environmental issues are not regularly included on the agenda of the governing board.

- About 40 percent of the organizations reported that they had paid fines or penalties for environmental violations in the past three years. Two-thirds of the respondents described their environmental risks as material.

5. The Environmental, Health, and Safety Auditing Roundtable (new name is The Auditing Roundtable) commissioned Richard L. Ratliff of Utah State University and a group of researchers to perform a study of environmental, health, and safety auditing. The researchers' findings related to the risk and independence issues are as follows.

   - The EH&S audit function is somewhat isolated from other organizational auditing activities. It is organized separately from internal auditing, only tangentially related to external audits of financial statements, and reports to an EH&S executive, rather than to the governing board or to senior management. This structure suggests that management believes EH&S auditing to be a technical field which is best placed within the EH&S function of the organization.

   - With that organizational placement, EH&S auditors could be unable to maintain their independence, which is considered one of the principal requirements of an effective audit function. EH&S audit managers typically report administratively to the executives who are responsible for the physical facilities being audited. Thus, poor EH&S performance would reflect badly on the facilities management team, who would therefore try to exercise their authority and influence over what is reported in audit findings, how audits are conducted, or what is included in the audit plan. This potential subordination of the auditors' professional judgment, even when only apparent, violates auditor independence and objectivity.

   - It is also common for written audit reports to be distributed no higher in the organization than to senior environmental executives. Those executives may have a potential conflict of interest, and they may curtail further distribution of EH&S audit findings to senior management and the governing board.

- Audit information is often classified as either (a) attorney-client privilege or attorney work product, (b) secret and confidential, or (c) if not confidential, then closely held. This results in severely restricted access to EH&S audit information.

Suggestions for the Chief Audit Executive

6. The CAE should foster a close working relationship with the chief environmental officer and coordinate activities with the plan for environmental auditing. In those instances where the environmental audit function reports to someone other than the CAE, the CAE should offer to review the audit plan and the performance of engagements. Periodically, the CAE should schedule a quality assurance review of the environmental audit function if it is organizationally independent of the internal audit activity. That review should determine if the environmental risks are being adequately addressed. An EH&S audit program could be either (a) compliance-focused (i.e., verifying compliance with laws, regulations, and the entity's own EH&S policies, procedures, and performance objectives) or (b) management systems-focused (i.e., providing assessments of management systems intended to ensure compliance with legal and internal requirements and the mitigation of risks), or (c) a combination of both approaches.

7. The CAE should evaluate whether the environmental auditors, who are not part of the CAE's organization, are in compliance with recognized professional auditing standards and a recognized code of ethics. The Board of Environmental, Health, & Safety Auditor Certifications (BEAC) as well as The IIA publish practice standards and ethical codes.

8. The CAE should evaluate the organizational placement and independence of the environmental audit function to ensure that significant matters resulting from serious risks to the enterprise are reported up the chain of command to the audit or other committee of the governing board. CAE should also facilitate the reporting of significant EH&S risk and control issues to the audit (or other board) committee.

Practice Advisory 2100-8: Internal Auditing's Role in Evaluating an Organization's Privacy Framework

**Interpretation of *Standard 2100* from the
*International Standards for the
Professional Practice of Internal Auditing***

Related Standard
2100 – Nature of Work
The internal audit activity should evaluate and contribute to the improvement of risk management, control, and governance processes using a systematic and disciplined approach.

Nature of this Practice Advisory: Internal auditors should consider the following suggestions when evaluating an organization's activities related to its privacy framework. This guidance is not intended to represent all the procedures necessary for a comprehensive assurance or consulting engagement related to the privacy framework, but rather a recommended core set of high level auditor responsibilities to complement related board and management responsibilities.

1. Concerns relating to the protection of personal privacy are becoming more apparent, focused, and global as advancements in information technology and communications continually introduce new risks and threats to privacy. Privacy controls are legal requirements for doing business in most of the world.

2. Privacy definitions vary widely depending upon country, culture, political environment, and legal framework. Privacy can encompass personal privacy (physical and psychological); privacy of space (freedom from surveillance); privacy of communication (freedom from monitoring); and privacy of information (collection, use, and disclosure of personal information by others). Personal information generally refers to information that can be associated with a specific individual, or that has identifying characteristics that might be combined with other information to do so.[1] It can include any factual or subjective information, recorded or not, in any form or media. Personal information might include, for example:
    *   Name, address, identification numbers, income, or blood type;
    *   Evaluations, comments, social status, or disciplinary actions; and
    *   Employee files, credit records, loan records.

3. Privacy is a risk management issue. Failure to protect privacy and personal information with the appropriate controls can have significant consequences for an organization. For example, it can damage the reputation of individuals and the organization, lead to legal liability issues, and contribute to consumer and employee mistrust.

4. There are a variety of laws and regulations developing worldwide relating to the protection of personal information. As well, there are generally accepted policies and practices that can be applied to the privacy issue.

5. It is clear that good privacy practices contribute to good governance and accountability. The governing body (e.g., the

---

[1]Hargraves, Kim, Susan B. Lione, Kerry L. Shackelford, and Peter C. Tilton, *Privacy: Assessing the Risk* (Altamonte Springs, FL: The Institute of Internal Auditors Research Foundation, 2003).

board of directors, head of an agency or legislative body) is ultimately accountable for ensuring that the principal risks of the organization have been identified and the appropriate systems have been implemented to mitigate those risks. This includes establishing the necessary privacy framework for the organization and monitoring its implementation.

6. The internal auditor can contribute to ensuring good governance and accountability by playing a role in helping an organization meet its privacy objectives. The internal auditor is uniquely positioned to evaluate the privacy framework in their organization and identify the significant risks along with the appropriate recommendations for their mitigation.

7. In conducting such an evaluation of the privacy framework, the internal auditor should consider the following:
    - The various laws, regulations, and policies relating to privacy in their respective jurisdictions (including any jurisdiction where the organization conducts business);
    - Liaison with in-house legal counsel to determine the exact nature of such laws, regulations, and other standards and practices applicable to the organization and the country/ countries in which it does business;
    - Liaison with information technology specialists to ensure information security and data protection controls are in place and regularly reviewed and assessed for appropriateness;
    - The level or maturity of the organization's privacy practices. Depending upon the level, the internal auditor may have differing roles. The auditor may facilitate the development and implementation of the privacy program, conduct a privacy risk assessment to determine the needs and risk exposures of the organization, or may review and provide assurance on the effectiveness of the privacy policies, practices, and controls across the organization. If the internal auditor

assumes a portion of the responsibility for developing and implementing a privacy program, the auditor's independence may be impaired.

8. Typically, the internal auditor could be expected to identify the types and appropriateness of information gathered by their organization that is deemed personal or private, the collection methodology used, and whether the organization's use of the information so collected is in accordance with its intended use and the laws, in the areas that the information is gathered, held, and used.

9. Given the highly technical and legal nature of the topic, the internal auditor should ensure that the appropriate in-depth knowledge and capacity to conduct any such evaluation of the privacy framework is available, using third-party experts, if necessary.

Practice Advisory 2110-1: Assessing the Adequacy of Risk Management Processes

Interpretation of *Standard 2110* from the *International Standards for the Professional Practice of Internal Auditing*

Related Standard
2110 – Risk Management
The internal audit activity should assist the organization by identifying and evaluating significant exposures to risk and contributing to the improvement of risk management and control systems.

Nature of this Practice Advisory: Internal auditors may be charged with the responsibility for providing assurance to management and the audit committee on the adequacy of the organization's risk management processes. This responsibility would require the auditor to formulate an opinion on whether the organization's risk management process is sufficient to protect the assets, reputation, and ongoing operations of the organization. This advisory provides guidance on the major risk management objectives that the auditor should consider in formulating an opinion on the adequacy of the organization's risk management process. This practice advisory covers only the assessment and reporting of the effectiveness of the organization's risk management process. Other Practice Advisories will address controls and consulting issues in greater depth. This advisory recognizes that an organization's risk management process is an important business process that can and should be evaluated in a manner similar to other strategically important processes.

1. Risk management is a key responsibility of management. To achieve its business objectives, management should ensure that sound risk management processes are in place and functioning. Boards and audit committees have an oversight role to determine that appropriate risk management processes are in place and that these processes are adequate and effective. Internal auditors should assist both management and the audit committee by examining, evaluating, reporting, and recommending improvements on the adequacy and effectiveness of management's risk processes. Management and the board are responsible for their organization's risk management and control processes. However, internal auditors acting in a consulting role can assist the organization in identifying, evaluating, and implementing risk management methodologies and controls to address those risks.

2. Developing assessments and reports on the organization's risk management processes are normally a high audit priority. Evaluating management's risk processes is different than the requirement that auditors use risk analysis to plan audits. However, information from a comprehensive risk management process, including the identification of management and board concerns, can assist the internal auditor in planning audit activities.

3. Each organization may choose a particular methodology to implement its risk management process. The internal auditor should ascertain whether the methodology is understood by key groups or individuals involved in corporate governance, including the board and audit committee. Internal auditors must satisfy themselves that the organization's risk management processes address five key objectives to formulate an opinion on the overall

adequacy of the risk management processes. The five key objectives of a risk management process are:

- Risks arising from business strategies and activities are identified and prioritized.
- Management and the board have determined the level of risks acceptable to the organization, including the acceptance of risks designed to accomplish the organization's strategic plans.
- Risk mitigation activities are designed and implemented to reduce, or otherwise manage, risk at levels that were determined to be acceptable to management and the board.
- Ongoing monitoring activities are conducted to periodically reassess risk and the effectiveness of controls to manage risk.
- The board and management receive periodic reports of the results of the risk management processes. The corporate governance processes of the organization should provide periodic communication of risks, risk strategies, and controls to stakeholders.

4. Internal auditors should recognize that there could be significant variations in the techniques used by various organizations for their risk management practices. Risk management processes should be designed for the nature of an organization's activities. Depending on the size and complexity of the organization's business activities, risk management processes can be:

- Formal or informal.
- Quantitative or subjective.
- Embedded in the business units or centralized at a corporate level.

The specific process used by an organization must fit that organization's culture, management style, and business objectives. For example, the use of derivatives or other sophisticated capital markets products by the organization would require the use of quantitative risk management tools. Smaller, less complex organizations may use an informal risk committee to discuss the organization's risk profile and to initiate periodic actions. The auditor should determine that the methodology chosen is both comprehensive and appropriate for the nature of the organization's activities.

5. Internal auditors should obtain sufficient evidence to satisfy themselves that the five key objectives of the risk management processes are being met in order to form an opinion on the adequacy of risk management processes. In gathering such evidence, the internal auditor should consider the following types of audit procedures:

- Research and review reference materials and background information on risk management methodologies as a basis to assess whether or not the process used by the organization is appropriate and represents best practices for the industry.
- Research and review current developments, trends, industry information related to the business conducted by the organization, and other appropriate sources of information to determine risks and exposures that may affect the organization and related control procedures used to address, monitor, and reassess those risks.
- Review corporate policies, board, and audit committee minutes to determine the organization's business strategies, risk management philosophy and methodology, appetite for risk, and acceptance of risks.
- Review previous risk evaluation reports by management, internal auditors, external auditors, and any other sources that may have issued such reports.
- Conduct interviews with line and executive management to determine business unit objectives, related risks, and management's risk mitigation and control monitoring activities.

- Assimilate information to independently evaluate the effectiveness of risk mitigation, monitoring, and communication of risks and associated control activities.
- Assess the appropriateness of reporting lines for risk monitoring activities.
- Review the adequacy and timeliness of reporting on risk management results.
- Review the completeness of management's risk analysis, actions taken to remedy issues raised by risk management processes, and suggest improvements.
- Determine the effectiveness of management's self-assessment processes through observations, direct tests of control and monitoring procedures, testing the accuracy of information used in monitoring activities, and other appropriate techniques.

  Review risk-related issues that may indicate weakness in risk management practices and, as appropriate, discuss with management, the audit committee, and the board of directors. If the auditor believes that management has accepted a level of risk that is inconsistent with the organization's risk management strategy and policies, or that is deemed unacceptable to the organization, the auditor should refer to *Standard 2600* on Management's Acceptance of Risks, and any related guidance for additional direction.

Practice Advisory 2110-2:
Internal Auditing's Role in the
Business Continuity Process

Interpretation of *Standard 2110* **from the**
International Standards for the
Professional Practice of Internal Auditing

Related Standard
2110 – Risk Management
The internal audit activity should assist the organization by identifying and evaluating significant exposures to risk and contributing to the improvement of risk management and control systems.

Nature of this Practice Advisory: *Internal auditors should consider the following suggestions when evaluating an organization's activities related to business continuity. Many processes are required to ensure the continuity of an organization after a disaster occurs. The development of a comprehensive plan begins with assessing the potential impact and consequences of a disaster and understanding the risks. (The entire process of ensuring business continuity will incorporate, among other things, business continuity and disaster recovery plans.) Those plans should be constructed, maintained, tested, and audited to ensure that it remains appropriate for the needs of the organization.*

1. Business interruption can result from natural occurrences and accidental or deliberate criminal acts. Those interruptions can have significant financial and operational ramifications. Auditors

should evaluate the organization's readiness to deal with business interruptions. A comprehensive plan would provide for emergency response procedures, alternative communication systems and site facilities, information systems backup, disaster recovery, business impact assessments and resumption plans, procedures for restoring utility services, and maintenance procedures for ensuring the readiness of the organization in the event of an emergency or disaster.

2. Internal auditing activity should assess the organization's business continuity planning process on a regular basis to ensure that senior management is aware of the state of disaster preparedness.

3. Many organizations do not expect to experience an interruption or lengthy delay of normal business processes and operations due to a disaster or other unforeseen event. Many business experts say that it is not *if* a disaster will occur, but *when* it will occur. Over time, an organization will experience an event that will result in the loss of information, access to properties (tangible or intangible), or the services of personnel. Exposure to those types of risks and the planning for business continuity is an integral part of an organization's risk management process. Advance planning is necessary to minimize the loss and ensure continuity of an organization's critical business functions. It may enable the organization to maintain an acceptable level of service to its stakeholders.

4. A crucial element of business recovery is the existence of a comprehensive and current disaster recovery plan. Internal auditors can play a role in the organization's planning for disaster recovery. Internal audit activity can (a) assist with the risk analysis, (b) evaluate the design and comprehensiveness of the plan after it has been drawn up, and (c) perform periodic assurance engagements to verify that the plan is kept up to date.

Planning

5. Organizations rely upon internal auditors for analysis of operations and assessment of risk management and control processes. Internal auditors acquire an understanding of the overall business operations and the individual functions and how they interrelate with one another. This positions the internal audit activity as a valuable resource in evaluating the disaster recovery plan during its formulation process.

6. Internal audit activity can help with an assessment of an organization's internal and external environment. Internal factors that may be considered include the turnover of management and changes in information systems, controls, and major projects and programs. External factors may include changes in outside regulatory and business environment and changes in markets and competitive conditions, international financial and economic conditions, and technologies. Internal auditors can help identify risks involving critical business activities and prioritize functions for recovery purposes.

Evaluation

7. Internal auditors can make a contribution as objective participants when they review the proposed business continuity and disaster recovery plans for design, completeness, and overall adequacy. The auditor can examine the plan to determine that it reflects the operations that have been included and evaluated in the risk assessment process and contains sufficient internal control concerns and prescriptions. The internal auditor's comprehensive knowledge of the organization's business operations and applications enables it to assist during the development phase of the business continuity plan by evaluating its organization, comprehensiveness, and recommended actions to manage risks and maintain effective controls during a recovery period.

Periodic Assurance Engagements

8. Internal auditors should periodically audit the organization's business continuity and disaster recovery plans. The audit objective is to verify that the plans are adequate to ensure the timely resumption of operations and processes after adverse circumstances, and that it reflects the current business-operating environment.

9. Business continuity and disaster recovery plans can become outdated very quickly. Coping with and responding to changes is an inevitable part of the task of management. Turnover of managers and executives and changes in system configurations, interfaces, and software can have a major impact on these plans. Internal audit activity should examine the recovery plan to determine whether (a) it is structured to incorporate important changes that could take place over time and (b) the revised plan will be communicated to the appropriate people, inside and outside the organization.

10. During the audit, internal auditors should consider:
    - Are all plans up to date? Do procedures exist for updating the plans?
    - Are all critical business functions and systems covered by the plans? If not, are the reasons for omissions documented?
    - Are the plans based on the risks and potential consequences of business interruptions?
    - Are the plans fully documented and in accordance with organizational policies and procedures? Have functional responsibilities been assigned?
    - Is the organization capable of and prepared to implement the plans?
    - Are the plans tested and revised based on the results?
    - Are the plans stored properly and safely? Is the location of and access to the plans known to management?

- Are the locations of alternate facilities (backup sites) known to employees?
- Do the plans call for coordination with local emergency services?

Internal Audit's Role After a Disaster

11. There is an important role for the internal auditors to play immediately after a disaster occurs. An organization is more vulnerable after a disaster has occurred, and it is trying to recover. During that recovery period, internal auditors should monitor the effectiveness of the recovery and control of operations. Internal audit activity should identify areas where internal controls and mitigating actions should be improved, and recommend improvements to the entity's business continuity plan. Internal audit can also provide support during the recovery activities.

12. After the disaster, usually within several months, internal auditors can assist in identifying the lessons learned from the disaster and the recovery operations. Those observations and recommendations may enhance activities to recover resources and update the next version of the business continuity plan.

13. In the final analysis, it is senior management that will determine the degree of the internal auditor's involvement in the business continuity and disaster recovery processes, considering their knowledge, skills, independence, and objectivity.

Practice Advisory 2120.A1-1: Assessing and Reporting on Control Processes

**Interpretation of *Standard 2120.A1* from the
*International Standards for the
Professional Practice of Internal Auditing***

Related Standard
2120.A1 – Based on the results of the risk assessment, the internal audit activity should evaluate the adequacy and effectiveness of controls encompassing the organization's governance, operations, and information systems. This should include:
- Reliability and integrity of financial and operational information.
- Effectiveness and efficiency of operations.
- Safeguarding of assets.
- Compliance with laws, regulations, and contracts.

Nature of this Practice Advisory: Internal auditors should consider the following guidance when assessing the effectiveness of an organization's system of controls and reporting that judgment to senior management and the board of directors. The audit work performed during the year should obtain sufficient information to enable an evaluation of the system of controls and the formulation of an opinion.

1. One of the tasks of a board of directors is to establish and maintain the organization's governance processes and to obtain assurances

concerning the effectiveness of the risk management and control processes. Senior management's role is to oversee the establishment, administration, and assessment of that system of risk management and control processes. The purpose of that multifaceted system of control processes is to support people of the organization in the management of risks and the achievement of the established and communicated objectives of the enterprise. More specifically, those control processes are expected to ensure, among other things, that the following conditions exist:

- Financial and operational information is reliable and possesses integrity.
- Operations are performed efficiently and achieve effective results.
- Assets are safeguarded.
- Actions and decisions of the organization are in compliance with laws, regulations, and contracts.

2. Among the responsibilities of the organization's managers is the assessment of the control processes in their respective areas. Internal and external auditors provide varying degrees of assurance about the state of effectiveness of the risk management and control processes in select activities and functions of the organization.

3. Senior management and the board normally expect that the chief audit executive (CAE) will perform sufficient audit work and gather other available information during the year so as to form a judgment about the adequacy and effectiveness of the risk management and control processes. The CAE should communicate that overall judgment about the organization's risk management process and system of controls to senior management and the audit committee. A growing number of organizations have included a management's report on the risk management process and system of internal controls in their annual or periodic reports to external stakeholders.

4. The CAE should develop a proposed audit plan normally for the coming year that ensures sufficient evidence will be obtained to evaluate the effectiveness of the risk management and control processes. The plan should call for audit engagements or other procedures to gather relevant information about all major operating units and business functions. It should include a review of the major risk management processes operating across the organization and a selection of the key risks identified from those processes. The audit plan should also give special consideration to those operations most affected by recent or expected changes. Those changes in circumstances may result from marketplace or investment conditions, acquisitions and divestitures, or restructures and new ventures. The proposed plan should be flexible so that adjustments may be made during the year as a result of changes in management strategies, external conditions, major risk areas, or revised expectations about achieving the organization's objectives.

5. In determining the proposed audit plan, the CAE should consider relevant work that will be performed by others. To minimize duplication and inefficiencies, the work planned or recently completed by management in its assessments of the risk management process, controls, and quality improvement processes as well as the work planned by the external auditors should be considered in determining the expected coverage of the audit plan for the coming year.

6. Finally, the CAE should evaluate the coverage of the proposed plan from two viewpoints: adequacy across organizational entities and inclusion of a variety of transaction and business-process types. If the scope of the proposed audit plan is insufficient to enable the expression of assurance about the organization's risk management and control processes, the CAE should inform senior management and the board of the expected deficiency, its causes, and the probable consequences.

7. The challenge for internal audit is to evaluate the effectiveness of the organization's system of risk management and controls based on the aggregation of many individual assessments. Those assessments are largely gained from internal audit engagements, management's self-assessments, and external auditor's work. As the engagements progress, internal auditors should communicate, on a timely basis, the findings to the appropriate levels of management so that prompt action can be taken to correct or mitigate the consequences of discovered control discrepancies or weaknesses.

8. Three key considerations in reaching an evaluation of the overall effectiveness of the organization's risk management and control processes are:
    *   Were significant discrepancies or weaknesses discovered from the audit work performed and other assessment information gathered?
    *   If so, were corrections or improvements made after the discoveries?
    *   Do the discoveries and their consequences lead to the conclusion that a pervasive condition exists resulting in an unacceptable level of business risk?

    The temporary existence of a significant risk management and control discrepancy or weakness does not necessarily lead to the judgment that it is pervasive and poses an unacceptable residual risk. The pattern of discoveries, degree of intrusion, and level of consequences and exposures are factors to be considered in determining whether the effectiveness of the whole system of controls is jeopardized and unacceptable risks exist.

9. The report of the CAE on the state of the organization's risk management and control processes should be presented, usually once a year, to senior management and the board. The report should emphasize the critical role played by the risk management and control processes in the quest for the organization's

objectives, and it should refer to major work performed by internal audit and to other important sources of information that were used to formulate the overall assurance judgment. The opinion section of the report is normally expressed in terms of negative assurance; that is, the audit work performed for the period and other information gathered did not disclose any significant weaknesses in the risk management and control processes that have a pervasive effect. If the risk management and control deficiencies or weaknesses are significant and pervasive, the assurance section of the report may be a qualified or adverse opinion, depending on the projected increase in the level of residual risk and its impact on the organization's objectives.

10. The target audiences for the annual report are senior executives and board members. Because these readers have divergent understandings of auditing and business, the CAE's annual report should be clear, concise, and informative. It should be composed and edited to be understandable by them and targeted to meet their informational needs. Its value to these readers can be enhanced by focusing on the major risk areas and including major recommendations for improvement and information about current control issues and trends, such as technology and information security exposures, patterns of control discrepancies or weaknesses across business units, and potential difficulties in complying with laws or regulations.

11. Ample evidence exists of an "expectation gap" surrounding the internal audit activity's work in evaluating and providing assurance about the state of risk management and control processes. One such gap exists between management and the board's normally high expectations about the value of internal auditing services and the internal auditor's more modest expectations that derive from knowledge of practical limitations on audit coverage and from self-doubt about generating sufficient evidence to support an informed and objective judgment. The CAE should be mindful

of the possible gap between what the report reader presumes and what actually happened during the year. He or she should use the report as another way to address different mental models and to suggest improving the capacity of the function or reducing the constraints to access and audit effectiveness.

Practice Advisory 2120.A1-2:
Using Control Self-assessment for
Assessing the Adequacy of Control Processes

Interpretation of *Standard 2120.A1* from the
International Standards for the
Professional Practice of Internal Auditing

Related Standard

2120.A1 – Based on the results of the risk assessment, the internal audit activity should evaluate the adequacy and effectiveness of controls encompassing the organization's governance, operations, and information systems. This should include:

- Reliability and integrity of financial and operational information.
- Effectiveness and efficiency of operations.
- Safeguarding of assets.
- Compliance with laws, regulations, and contracts.

Nature of this Practice Advisory: Control self-assessment (CSA) methodology can be used by managers and internal auditors for assessing the adequacy of the organization's risk management and control processes. Internal auditors can utilize CSA programs for gathering relevant information about risks and controls, for focusing the audit plan on high risk, unusual areas, and to forge greater collaboration with operating managers and work teams.

1. Senior management is charged with overseeing the establishment, administration, and evaluation of the processes of risk

management and control. Operating managers' responsibilities include assessment of the risks and controls in their units. Internal and external auditors provide varying degrees of assurance about the state of effectiveness of the risk management and control processes of the organization. Both managers and auditors have an interest in using techniques and tools that sharpen the focus and expand the efforts to assess risk management and control processes that are in place and to identify ways to improve their effectiveness.

2. A methodology encompassing self-assessment surveys and facilitated workshops called CSA is a useful and efficient approach for managers and internal auditors to collaborate in assessing and evaluating control procedures. In its purest form, CSA integrates business objectives and risks with control processes. Control self-assessment is also referred to as "Control/risk self-assessment" or "CRSA." Although CSA practitioners use a number of differing techniques and formats, most implemented programs share some key features and goals. An organization that uses self-assessment will have a formal, documented process that allows management and work teams, who are directly involved in a business unit, function, or process to participate in a structured manner for the purpose of:
    *   Identifying risks and exposures;
    *   Assessing the control processes that mitigate or manage those risks;
    *   Developing action plans to reduce risks to acceptable levels; and
    *   Determining the likelihood of achieving the business objectives.

3. The outcomes that may be derived from self-assessment methodologies are:
    *   People in business units become trained and experienced in assessing risks and associating control processes with

managing those risks and improving the chances of achieving business objectives.

- Informal, "soft" controls are more easily identified and evaluated.
- People are motivated to take "ownership" of the control processes in their units and corrective actions taken by the work teams are often more effective and timely.
- The entire objectives-risks-controls infrastructure of an organization is subject to greater monitoring and continuous improvement.
- Internal auditors become involved in and knowledgeable about the self-assessment process by serving as facilitators, scribes, and reporters for the work teams and as trainers of risk and control concepts supporting the CSA program.
- Internal audit activity acquires more information about the control processes within the organization and can leverage that additional information in allocating their scarce resources so as to spend a greater effort in investigating and performing tests of business units or functions that have significant control weaknesses or high residual risks.
- Management's responsibility for the risk management and control processes of the organization is reinforced, and managers will be less tempted to abdicate those activities to specialists, such as auditors.
- The primary role of the internal audit activity will continue to include the validation of the evaluation process by performing tests and the expression of its professional judgment on the adequacy and effectiveness of the whole risk management and control systems.

4. The wide variety of approaches used for CSA processes in organizations reflects the differences in industry, geography, structure, organizational culture, degree of employee empowerment, dominant management style, and the manner of formulating strategies and policies. That observation suggests

that the success of a particular type of CSA program in one enterprise may not be replicated in another organization. The CSA process should be customized to fit the unique characteristics of each organization. Also, it suggests that a CSA approach needs to be dynamic and change with the continual development of the organization.

5. The three primary forms of CSA programs are facilitated team workshops, surveys, and management-produced analysis. Organizations often combine more than one approach.

6. Facilitated team workshops gather information from work teams representing different levels in the business unit or function. The format of the workshop may be based on objectives, risks, controls, or processes.
    *   Objective-based format focuses on the best way to accomplish a business objective. The workshop begins by identifying the controls presently in place to support the objective and then determining the residual risks remaining. The aim of the workshop is to decide whether the control procedures are working effectively and are resulting in residual risks within an acceptable level.
    *   Risk-based format focuses on listing the risks to achieving an objective. The workshop begins by listing all possible barriers, obstacles, threats, and exposures that might prevent achieving an objective and then examining the control procedures to determine if they are sufficient to manage the key risks. The aim of the workshop is to determine significant residual risks. This format takes the work team through the entire objective-risks-controls formula.
    *   Control-based format focuses on how well the controls in place are working. This format is different than the two above because the facilitator identifies the key risks and controls before the beginning of the workshop. During the workshop, the work team assesses how well the controls

mitigate risks and promote the achievement of objectives. The aim of the workshop is to produce an analysis of the gap between how controls are working and how well management expects those controls to work.

- Process-based format focuses on selected activities that are elements of a chain of processes. The processes are usually a series of related activities that go from some beginning point to an end, such as the various steps in purchasing, product development, or revenue generation. This type of workshop usually covers the identification of the objectives of the whole process and the various intermediate steps. The aim of the workshop is to evaluate, update, validate, improve, and streamline the whole process and its component activities. This workshop format may have a greater breadth of analysis than a control-based approach by covering multiple objectives within the process and supporting concurrent management efforts, such as reengineering, quality improvement, and continuous improvement initiatives.

7. The survey form of CSA utilizes a questionnaire that tends to ask mostly simple "Yes-No" or "Have-Have Not" questions that are carefully written to be understood by the target recipients. Surveys are often used if the desired respondents are too numerous or widely dispersed to participate in a workshop. They are also preferred if the culture in the organization may hinder open, candid discussions in workshop settings or if management desires to minimize the time spent and costs incurred in gathering the information.

8. The form of self-assessment called "management-produced analyses" covers most other approaches by management groups to produce information about selected business processes, risk management activities, and control procedures. The analysis is often intended to reach an informed and timely judgment about specific characteristics of control procedures and is commonly

prepared by a team in staff or support role. The internal auditor may synthesize this analysis with other information to enhance the understanding about controls and to share the knowledge with managers in business or functional units as part of the organization's CSA program.

9. All self-assessment programs are based on managers and members of the work teams possessing an understanding of risks and controls concepts and using those concepts in communications. For training sessions, to facilitate the orderly flow of workshop discussions and as a check on the completeness of the overall process, organizations often use a control framework such as the COSO and COCO models.

10. In the typical CSA facilitated workshop, a report will be largely created during the deliberations. A group consensus will be recorded for the various segments of the discussions, and the group will review the proposed final report before the end of the final session. Some programs will use anonymous voting techniques to ensure the free flow of information and viewpoints during the workshops and to aid in negotiating differences between viewpoints and interest groups.

11. Internal audit's investment in some CSA programs is fairly significant. It may sponsor, design, implement, and, in effect, own the process, conducting the training, supplying the facilitators, scribes, and reporters, and orchestrating the participation of management and work teams. In other CSA programs, internal audit's involvement is minimal, serving as interested party and consultant of the whole process and as ultimate verifier of the evaluations produced by the teams. In most programs, internal audit's investment in the organization's CSA efforts is somewhere between the two extremes described above. As the level of internal audit's involvement in the CSA program and individual workshop deliberations increases, the chief audit executive should

monitor the objectivity of the internal audit staff, take steps to manage that objectivity (if necessary), and augment internal audit testing to ensure that bias or partiality do not affect the final judgments of the staff. *Standard 1120* states: "Internal auditors should have an impartial, unbiased attitude and avoid conflicts of interest."

12. A CSA program augments the traditional role of internal audit activity by assisting management in fulfilling its responsibilities to establish and maintain risk management and control processes and to evaluate the adequacy of that system. Through a CSA program, the internal audit activity and the business units and functions collaborate to produce better information about how well the control processes are working and how significant the residual risks are.

13. Although providing staff support for the CSA program as facilitator and specialist, the internal audit activity often finds that it may reduce the effort spent in gathering information about control procedures and eliminate some testing. A CSA program should increase the coverage of assessing control processes across the organization, improve the quality of corrective actions made by the process owners, and focus internal audit's work on reviewing high-risk processes and unusual situations. It can focus on validating the evaluation conclusions produced by the CSA process, synthesizing the information gathered from the components of the organization, and expressing its overall judgment about the effectiveness of controls to senior management and the audit committee.

Practice Advisory 2120.A1-3: Internal Auditing's Role in Quarterly Financial Reporting, Disclosures, and Management Certifications

Interpretation of *Standard 2120.A1* from the
International Standards for the
Professional Practice of Internal Auditing

Related Standard

2120.A1 – Based on the results of the risk assessment, the internal audit activity should evaluate the adequacy and effectiveness of controls encompassing the organization's governance, operations, and information systems. This should include:

- Reliability and integrity of financial and operational information.
- Effectiveness and efficiency of operations.
- Safeguarding of assets.
- Compliance with laws, regulations, and contracts.

Nature of this Practice Advisory: Internal auditors should consider the following guidance regarding quarterly financial reports, disclosures, and management certifications related to requirements of the U.S. Securities and Exchange Commission (SEC). While such requirements are specifically directed to U.S. registrants of the SEC, they are also applicable to over 1,300 foreign registrants. In order to provide a higher level of confidence to stakeholders, a growing number of non-publicly

held organizations are voluntarily adopting selected SEC
requirements to demonstrate best practices for disclosures and
controls over quarterly reporting. Internal auditors are also
directed to Practice Advisory 2120.A1, "Assessing and Reporting
on Control Processes," for additional guidance.

1. The strength of all financial markets depends on investor
    confidence. Events involving allegations of misdeeds by
    corporate executives, independent auditors, and other market
    participants have undermined that confidence. In response to
    this threat, the U.S. Congress and a growing number of legislative
    bodies and regulatory agencies in other countries passed
    legislation and regulation affecting corporate disclosures and
    financial reporting. Specifically in the United States of America
    the Sarbanes-Oxley Act of 2002 (the "Sarbanes-Oxley Act")
    enacted sweeping reform requiring additional disclosures and
    certifications of financial statements by principal executive and
    financial officers.

2. The new law challenges companies to devise processes that
    will permit senior officers to acquire the necessary assurances
    on which to base their personal certification. A key component
    of the certification process is the management of risk and internal
    controls over the recording and summarizing of financial
    information.

New Statutory Requirements

3. Section 302 of the Sarbanes-Oxley Act outlines the corporate
    responsibility for financial reports, and the SEC has issued
    guidance to implement the act. As adopted, SEC Rules 13a-14
    and 15d-14 require an issuer's principal executive officer or
    officers and the principal financial officer or officers, or persons
    performing similar functions, to certify in each quarterly and
    annual report, including transition reports, filed or submitted by

the issuer under Section 13(a) or 15(d) of the Exchange Act that:

- He or she has reviewed the report;
- Based on his or her knowledge, the report does not contain any untrue statement of a material fact or omit a material fact necessary to make a statement, in light of the circumstances under which such statements are made, not misleading with respect to the period covered by the report;
- Based on his or her knowledge, the financial statements, and other financial information included in the report, fairly present in all material respects the financial condition, results of operations and cash flows of the issuer as of, and for, the periods presented in the report;
- He or she and the other certifying officers:
  - Are responsible for establishing and maintaining "disclosure controls and procedures" (a newly defined term reflecting the concept of controls and procedures related to disclosure embodied in Section 302(a)(4) of the Act) for the issuer;
  - Have designed such disclosure controls and procedures to ensure that material information is made known to them, particularly during the period in which the periodic report is being prepared;
  - Have evaluated the effectiveness of the issuer's disclosure controls and procedures as of a date within 90 days prior to the filing date of the report; and
  - Have presented in the report their conclusions about the effectiveness of the disclosure controls and procedures based on the required evaluation as of that date;
- He or she and the other certifying officers have disclosed to the issuer's auditors and to the audit committee of the board of directors (or persons fulfilling the equivalent function):
  - All significant deficiencies in the design or operation of internal controls (a preexisting term relating to internal

controls regarding financial reporting) which could
adversely affect the issuer's ability to record, process,
summarize, and report financial data and have identified
for the issuer's auditors any material weaknesses in
internal controls; and

- Any fraud, whether or not material, that involves
  management or other employees who have a significant
  role in the issuer's internal controls; and
- Whether or not there were significant changes in internal
  controls or in other factors that could significantly affect
  internal controls subsequent to the date of their
  evaluation, including any corrective actions with regard
  to significant deficiencies and material weaknesses.

Recommended Actions for Internal Auditors

4. The following actions and considerations are offered to internal
    auditors as value-added services that can be provided regarding
    quarterly financial reports, disclosures, and management
    certifications related to requirements of the SEC and the
    Sarbanes-Oxley Act. These recommended actions are also
    offered as best practices to non-publicly held companies and
    other organizations seeking to adopt similar processes over
    quarterly financial reporting.
    a. The internal auditor's role in such processes may range from
        initial designer of the process, participant on a disclosure
        committee, coordinator or liaison between management and
        its auditors, to independent assessor of the process.
    b. All internal auditors involved in quarterly reporting and
        disclosure processes should have a clearly defined role and
        evaluate responsibilities with appropriate IIA Consulting and
        Assurance Standards, and with guidance contained in related
        Practice Advisories.
    c. Internal auditors should ensure that organizations have a
        formal policy and documented procedures to govern

processes for quarterly financial reports, related disclosures, and regulatory reporting requirements. Appropriate review of any policies and procedures by attorneys, external auditors, and other experts can offer additional comfort that policies and procedures are comprehensive and accurately reflect applicable requirements.

d. Internal auditors should encourage organizations to establish a "disclosure committee" to coordinate the process and provide oversight to participants. Representatives from key areas of the organization should be represented on the committee, including key financial managers, legal counsel, risk management, internal audit, and any area providing input or data for the regulatory filings and disclosures. Normally the chief audit executive (CAE) should be a member of the disclosure committee. Consideration should be given to CAE status on the committee. CAEs who serve as committee chairs or regular or "voting" members need to be aware of independence considerations and are advised to review IIA *Standards* and related Practice Advisories for guidance and required disclosures. Status as an "ex-officio" member normally would not create independence problems.

e. Internal auditors should periodically review and evaluate quarterly reporting and disclosure processes, disclosure committee activities, and related documentation, and provide management and the audit committee with an assessment of the process and assurance concerning overall operations and compliance with policies and procedures. Internal auditors whose independence may be impaired due to their assigned role in the process should ensure that management and the audit committee are able to obtain appropriate assurance about the process from other sources. Other sources can include internal self-assessments as well as third parties such as external auditors and consultants.

f. Internal auditors should recommend appropriate improvements to the policies, procedures, and process for quarterly reporting and related disclosures based on the results of an assessment of related activities. Recommended best practices for such activities may include all, or components of, the following tools and procedures, depending on the specific process used by each organization:

-   Properly documented policies, procedures, controls, and monitoring reports
-   Quarterly checklist of procedures and key control elements
-   Standardized control reports on key disclosure controls
-   Management self-assessments (such as CSA)
-   Sign-offs or representation statements from key managers
-   Review of draft regulatory filings prior to submission
-   Process maps to document the source of data elements for regulatory filings, key controls, and responsible parties for each element
-   Follow-up on previously reported outstanding items
-   Consideration of internal audit reports issued during the period
-   Special or specifically targeted reviews of high-risk, complex, and problem areas; including material accounting estimates, reserve valuations, off-balance sheet activities, major subsidiaries, joint ventures, and special purpose entities
-   Observation of the "closing process" for the financial statements and related adjusting entries, including waived adjustments
-   Conference calls with key management from remote locations to ensure appropriate consideration of and participation by all major components of the organization
-   Review of potential and pending litigation, and contingent liabilities
-   CAE report on internal control, issued at least annually, and possibly quarterly

  - Regularly scheduled disclosure and audit committee meetings
g. Internal auditors should compare processes for complying with Section 302 of the Sarbanes-Oxley Act (quarterly financial reporting and disclosures) to procedures developed to comply with Section 404 concerning management's annual assessment and public report on internal controls. Processes designed to be similar or compatible will contribute to operational efficiencies and reduce the likelihood or risk for problems and errors to occur or go undetected. While processes and procedures may be similar, it is possible that the internal auditor's role may vary. In some organizations the work of internal auditors may form the basis for management's assertions about internal control, while in other organizations internal auditors may be called upon to evaluate management's assessment.
  - The nature of internal audit's work, and use thereof, can potentially affect the treatment or degree of reliance placed upon the internal auditor's work by the external auditor. Internal auditors should ensure that each participant's role is clarified and activities are coordinated and agreed upon with management and the external auditors.
  - In organizations where management conducts its own assessment of controls as the basis for an opinion, internal auditors should evaluate management's assessment and supporting documentation.
  - Internal auditors should evaluate how internal audit report comments are classified and ensure that comments that may be subject to disclosure in quarterly certifications or the annual report on internal controls are appropriately communicated to management and the audit committee. Extra care should be taken to ensure such comments are adequately resolved in a timely manner.

Practice Advisory 2120.A1-4: Auditing the Financial Reporting Process

Interpretation of *Standard 2120.A1* from the *International Standards for the Professional Practice of Internal Auditing*

Related Standard

2120.A1 – Based on the results of the risk assessment, the internal audit activity should evaluate the adequacy and effectiveness of controls encompassing the organization's governance, operations, and information systems. This should include:

- Reliability and integrity of financial and operational information.
- Effectiveness and efficiency of operations.
- Safeguarding of assets.
- Compliance with laws, regulations, and contracts.

Nature of this Practice Advisory: This Practice Advisory explores internal audit's role and responsibilities in an organization's financial reporting process. The roles of senior management, external auditors, and internal auditors are:

- *Executive management is the owner of the control environment and financial information, including the notes accompanying the financial statements and the accompanying disclosures in the financial report.*
- *External auditor assures the financial report user that the reported information fairly presents the financial condition and result of operations of the organization*

in accordance with generally accepted accounting principles.
- *The internal auditor performs procedures to provide a level of assurance to senior management and the audit or other committee of the governing board that controls surrounding the processes supporting the development of financial report are effective.*

Practice Advisory 2060-2, "Relationship with the Audit Committee," covers the internal auditor's interactions with the audit committee. Practice Advisory 2120.A1-1, "Assessing and Reporting on Control Processes," discusses the evidence needed to assess a system of internal controls and form an opinion. Practice Advisory 2120.A1-3, "Internal Auditing's Role in Quarterly Financial Reporting, Disclosures, and Management Certifications," provides guidance on the requirements of U.S. Sarbanes-Oxley Act and the related rules of the U.S. Securities and Exchange Commission. This Practice Advisory focuses on internal auditor relationships with senior management and the external auditor regarding the financial reporting process.

1. The published reports of corporate governance failures in the United States of America and other countries underscore the need for change to achieve greater accountability and transparency by all organizations — profit making, nonprofit, and governmental. Senior management, boards of directors, internal auditors, and external auditors are the cornerstones of the foundation on which effective organizational governance is built. Internal audit activity plays a key role in support of good organizational governance; it has a unique position to assist in improving an organization's operations by evaluating and improving the effectiveness of risk management, control, and governance processes. Recent initiatives have put the spotlight on the need for senior management to be more accountable for the information contained in an organization's financial reports.

Senior management and the audit committee of many organizations are requesting additional services from the internal audit activity to improve the governance and financial reporting processes. These requests include evaluations of the organization's internal controls over financial reporting and the reliability and integrity of its financial reports.

Reporting on Internal Control

2. An organization's audit or other board committee and internal auditing activity have interlocking goals. The core role of the chief audit executive (CAE) is to ensure that the audit committee receives the support and assurance services it needs and requests. One of the primary objectives of the audit committee is oversight of the organization's financial reporting processes to ensure their reliability and fairness. The committee and senior management typically request that the internal audit activity perform sufficient audit work and gather other available information during the year to form an opinion on the adequacy and effectiveness of the internal control processes. The CAE normally communicates that overall evaluation, on a timely basis, to the committee. The committee will evaluate the coverage and adequacy of the CAE's report and may incorporate its conclusion in the committee's report to the governing board.

3. Internal audit activity's work plans and specific assurance engagements begin with a careful identification of the exposures facing the organization, and internal audit's work plan is based on the risks and the assessment of the risk management and controls processes maintained by management to mitigate those risks. Among the events and transactions included in the identification of risks are:
    *   New businesses — including mergers and acquisitions.
    *   New products and systems.

- Joint ventures and partnerships.
- Restructuring.
- Management estimates, budgets, and forecasts.
- Environmental matters.
- Regulatory compliance.

A Framework for Internal Control

4. The assessment of a system of internal control of an organization should employ a broad definition of control. The IIA believes that the most effective internal control guidance available today is the report *Internal Control – Integrated Framework*, published in 1992 and 1994 by the Committee of Sponsoring Organizations (COSO) of the Treadway Commission. While use of the COSO model is widely accepted, it may be appropriate to use some other recognized and credible model. Sometimes, regulatory or legal requirements will specify the use of a particular model or control design for an organization or industry within a country.

5. Several conclusions in the *Internal Control – Integrated Framework* report are relevant to this discussion.
    - Internal control is defined broadly; it is not limited to accounting controls and is not narrowly restricted to financial reporting.
    - While accounting and financial reports are important issues, there are other important aspects of the business, such as resource protection, operational efficiency and effectiveness, and compliance with rules, regulations, and organization policies. These factors also have an impact on financial reporting.
    - Internal control is management's responsibility and requires the participation of all persons within an organization if it is to be effective.

- The control framework is tied to the business objectives and is flexible enough to be adaptable.

Reporting on the Effectiveness of Internal Control

6. The CAE should provide to the audit committee the internal audit's assessment of the effectiveness of the organization's system of controls, including its judgment on the adequacy of the control model or design. A governing board must rely on management to maintain an adequate and effective internal control system. It will reinforce that reliance with independent oversight. The board or its audit (or other designated) committee should ask the following questions, and the CAE may be expected to assist in answering them.

   (a) Is there a strong ethical environment and culture?
      - Do board members and senior executives set examples of high integrity?
      - Are performance and incentive targets realistic or do they create the excessive pressure for short-term results?
      - Is the organization's code of conduct reinforced with training and top-down communication? Does the message reach the employees in the field?
      - Are the organization's communication channels open? Do all levels of management get the information they need?
      - Is there zero tolerance for fraudulent financial reporting at any level?

   (b) How does the organization identify and manage risks?
      - Is there a risk management process, and is it effective?
      - Is risk managed throughout the organization?
      - Are major risks candidly discussed with the board?

   (c) Is the control system effective?
      - Are the organization's controls over the financial reporting process comprehensive, including preparation

of financial statements, related notes, and the other required and discretionary disclosures that are an integral part of the financial reports?

- Do senior and line management demonstrate that they accept control responsibility?
- Is there an increasing frequency of "surprises" occurring at the senior management, board, or public levels from the organization's reported financial results or in the accompanying financial disclosures?
- Is there good communication and reporting throughout the organization?
- Are controls seen as enhancing the achievement of objectives or a "necessary evil"?
- Are qualified people hired promptly, and do they receive adequate training?
- Are problem areas fixed quickly and completely?

(d) Is there strong monitoring?

- Is the board independent of management, free of conflicts of interest, well informed, and inquisitive?
- Does internal audit have the support of senior management and the audit committee?
- Do the internal and external auditors have and use open lines of communication and private access to all members of senior management and the audit committee?
- Is line management monitoring the control process?
- Is there a program to monitor outsourced processes?

7. Internal controls cannot ensure success. Bad decisions, poor managers, or environmental factors can negate controls. Also, dishonest management may override controls and ignore or stifle communications from subordinates. An active and independent governing board that is coupled with open and truthful communications from all components of management and is assisted by capable financial, legal, and internal audit functions is capable of identifying problems and providing effective oversight.

Roles for the Internal Auditor

8. The CAE needs to review internal audit's risk assessment and audit plans for the year, if adequate resources have not been committed to helping senior management, the audit committee, and the external auditor with their responsibilities in the upcoming year's financial reporting regimentation. The financial reporting process encompasses the steps to create the information and prepare financial statements, related notes, and other accompanying disclosures in the organization's financial reports.

9. The CAE should allocate the internal audit's resources to the financial reporting, governance, and control processes consistent with the organization's risk assessment. The CAE should perform procedures that provide a level of assurance to senior management and the audit committee that controls surrounding the processes supporting the development of financial reports are adequately designed and effectively executed. The controls should be adequate to ensure the prevention and detection of significant errors, irregularities, incorrect assumptions and estimates, and other events that could result in inaccurate or misleading financial statements, related notes, or other disclosures.

10. The following lists suggested topics that the CAE may consider in supporting the organization's governance process and the oversight responsibilities of the governing board and its audit committee (or other designated committee) to ensure the reliability and integrity of financial reports.
    (a) Financial Reporting
        - Providing information relevant to the appointment of the independent accountants.
        - Coordinating audit plans, coverage, and scheduling with the external auditors.
        - Sharing audit results with the external auditors.

- Communicating pertinent observations with the external auditors and audit committee about accounting policies and policy decisions (including accounting decisions for discretionary items and off-balance sheet transactions), specific components of the financial reporting process, and unusual or complex financial transactions and events (e.g., related-party transactions, mergers and acquisitions, joint ventures, and partnership transactions).
- Participating in the financial reports and disclosures review process with the audit committee, external auditors, and senior management; evaluating the quality of the financial reports, including those filed with regulatory agencies.
- Assessing the adequacy and effectiveness of the organization's internal controls, specifically those controls over the financial reporting process; this assessment should consider the organization's susceptibility to fraud and the effectiveness of programs and controls to mitigate or eliminate those exposures.
- Monitoring management's compliance with the organization's code of conduct and ensuring that ethical policies and other procedures promoting ethical behavior are being followed; an important factor in establishing an effective ethical culture in the organization is when members of senior management set a good example of ethical behavior and provide open and truthful communications to employees, the board, and outside stakeholders.

(b) Corporate Governance
- Reviewing corporate policies relating to compliance with laws and regulations, ethics, conflict of interests, and the timely and thorough investigation of misconduct and fraud allegations.
- Reviewing pending litigation or regulatory proceedings bearing on organizational risk and governance.

- Providing information on employee conflicts of interest, misconduct, fraud, and other outcomes of the organization's ethical procedures and reporting mechanisms.

(c) Corporate Control

- Reviewing the reliability and integrity of the organization's operating and financial information compiled and reported by the organization.
- Performing an analysis of the controls for critical accounting policies and comparing them with preferred practices (e.g., transactions in which questions are raised about revenue recognition or off-balance sheet accounting treatment should be reviewed for compliance with appropriate generally accepted accounting standards).
- Evaluating the reasonableness of estimates and assumptions used in preparing operating and financial reports.
- Ensuring that estimates and assumptions included in disclosures or comments are in line with underlying organizational information and practices and with similar items reported by other companies, if appropriate.
- Evaluating the process of preparing, reviewing, approving, and posting journal entries.
- Evaluating the adequacy of controls in the accounting function.

Practice Advisory 2120.A4-1: Control Criteria

Interpretation of *Standard 2120.A4* from the *International Standards for the Professional Practice of Internal Auditing*

Related Standard
2120.A4 – Adequate criteria are needed to evaluate controls. Internal auditors should ascertain the extent to which management has established adequate criteria to determine whether objectives and goals have been accomplished. If adequate, internal auditors should use such criteria in their evaluation. If inadequate, internal auditors should work with management to develop appropriate evaluation criteria.

Nature of this Practice Advisory: Internal auditors should consider the following suggestions when evaluating control criteria. This guidance is not intended to represent all the considerations that may be necessary during such an evaluation, but simply a recommended set of items that should be addressed.

1. Before controls can be evaluated, management should determine the level of risk they want to take in the area to be reviewed. Internal auditors should identify what that level of risk is. This should be identified in terms of reducing the potential impact of the key threats to the achievement of the major objectives for the area under review.

2. If management has not identified the key risks and the level of risk they want to take, the internal auditors may be able to help

them through the facilitation of risk identification workshops or other techniques used by the organization.

3. Once the risk level is determined, the controls currently in place can be assessed to determine how successful they are expected to be in reducing the risk to the desired level.

Practice Advisory 2130-1: Role of the Internal Audit Activity and Internal Auditor in the Ethical Culture of an Organization

Interpretation of *Standard 2130* from the *International Standards for the Professional Practice of Internal Auditing*

Related Standard
2130 – Governance
The internal audit activity should assess and make appropriate recommendations for improving the governance process in its accomplishment of the following objectives:
- Promoting appropriate ethics and values within the organization.
- Ensuring effective organizational performance management and accountability.
- Effectively communicating risk and control information to appropriate areas of the organization.
- Effectively coordinating the activities of and communicating information among the board, external and internal auditors, and management.

Related Standard
2130.A1 – The internal audit activity should evaluate the design, implementation, and effectiveness of the organization's ethics-related objectives, programs, and activities.

Nature of this Practice Advisory: Internal auditors should consider the following in determining the role to play in the ethical culture of an organization. This role can vary depending on the existence, lack of, or degree of development of the organization's ethical culture. This guidance is not intended to represent all the procedures that may be necessary for a comprehensive assurance or consulting engagement related to an organization's ethics culture.

1. This Practice Advisory underscores the importance of organizational culture in establishing the ethical climate of an enterprise and suggests the role that internal auditors could play in improving that ethical climate. Specifically, the Practice Advisory:
   - Describes the nature of the governance process,
   - Links it to the ethical culture of the organization,
   - States that all people associated with the organization, and specifically internal auditors, should assume the role of ethics advocates, and
   - Lists the characteristics of an enhanced ethical culture.

Governance and Organizational Culture

2. An organization uses various legal forms, structures, strategies, and procedures to ensure that it:
   (a) Complies with society's legal and regulatory rules,
   (b) Satisfies the generally accepted business norms, ethical precepts, and social expectations of society,
   (c) Provides overall benefit to society and enhances the interests of the specific stakeholders in both the long- and short-term, and
   (d) Reports fully and truthfully to its owners, regulators, other stakeholders, and general public to ensure accountability for its decisions, actions, conduct, and performance.

The way in which an organization chooses to conduct its affairs to meet those four responsibilities is commonly referred to as its governance process. The organization's governing body (such as a board of directors or trustees or a managing board) and its senior management are accountable for the effectiveness of the governance process.

3. An organization's governance practices reflect a unique and ever-changing culture that affects roles, specifies behavior, sets goals and strategies, measures performance, and defines the terms of accountability. That culture impacts the values, roles, and behavior that will be articulated and tolerated by the organization and determines how sensitive — thoughtful or indifferent — the enterprise is in meeting its responsibilities to society. Thus, how effective the overall governance process is in performing its expected function largely depends on the organization's culture.

Shared Responsibility for the Organization's Ethical Culture

4. All people associated with the organization share some responsibility for the state of its ethical culture. Because of the complexity and dispersion of decision-making processes in most enterprises, each individual should be encouraged to be an ethics advocate, whether the role is delegated officially or merely conveyed informally. Codes of conduct and statements of vision and policy are important declarations of the organization's values and goals, the behavior expected of its people, and the strategies for maintaining a culture that aligns with its legal, ethical, and societal responsibilities. A growing number of organizations have designated a chief ethics officer as counselor of executives, managers, and others and as champion within the organization for "doing the right thing."

Internal Audit Activity as Ethics Advocate

5. Internal auditors and the internal audit activity should take an active role in support of the organization's ethical culture. They possess a high level of trust and integrity within the organization and the skills to be effective advocates of ethical conduct. They have the competence and capacity to appeal to the enterprise's leaders, managers, and other employees to comply with the legal, ethical, and societal responsibilities of the organization.

6. The internal audit activity may assume one of several different roles as an ethics advocate. Those roles include chief ethics officer (ombudsman, compliance officer, management ethics counselor, or ethics expert), member of an internal ethics council, or assessor of the organization's ethical climate. In some circumstances, the role of chief ethics officer may conflict with the independence attribute of the internal audit activity.

Assessment of the Organization's Ethical Climate

7. At a minimum, the internal audit activity should periodically assess the state of the ethical climate of the organization and the effectiveness of its strategies, tactics, communications, and other processes in achieving the desired level of legal and ethical compliance. Internal auditors should evaluate the effectiveness of the following features of an enhanced, highly effective ethical culture:
   (a) Formal Code of Conduct, which is clear and understandable, and related statements, policies (including procedures covering fraud and corruption), and other expressions of aspiration.
   (b) Frequent communications and demonstrations of expected ethical attitudes and behavior by the influential leaders of the organization.

(c) Explicit strategies to support and enhance the ethical culture with regular programs to update and renew the organization's commitment to an ethical culture.

(d) Several, easily accessible ways for people to confidentially report alleged violations of the Code, policies, and other acts of misconduct.

(e) Regular declarations by employees, suppliers, and customers that they are aware of the requirements for ethical behavior in transacting the organization's affairs.

(f) Clear delegation of responsibilities to ensure that ethical consequences are evaluated, confidential counseling is provided, allegations of misconduct are investigated, and case findings are properly reported.

(g) Easy access to learning opportunities to enable all employees to be ethics advocates.

(h) Positive personnel practices that encourage every employee to contribute to the ethical climate of the organization.

(i) Regular surveys of employees, suppliers, and customers to determine the state of the ethical climate in the organization.

(j) Regular reviews of the formal and informal processes within the organization that could potentially create pressures and biases that would undermine the ethical culture.

(k) Regular reference and background checks as part of hiring procedures, including integrity tests, drug screening, and similar measures.

Practice Advisory 2200-1:
Engagement Planning

Interpretation of *Standard 2200* from the
International Standards for the
Professional Practice of Internal Auditing

Related Standard
2200 – Engagement Planning
Internal auditors should develop and record a plan for each engagement, including the scope, objectives, timing, and resource allocations.

Related Standard
2201 – Planning Considerations
In planning the engagement, internal auditors should consider:
- The objectives of the activity being reviewed and the means by which the activity controls its performance and achievement of those objectives.
- The significant risks to the activity, its objectives, resources, and operations and the means by which the potential impact and/or likelihood of risk is kept to an acceptable level.
- The adequacy and effectiveness of the activity's risk management and control systems compared to a relevant control framework or model.
- The opportunities for making significant improvements to the activities risk management and control systems.

Nature of this Practice Advisory: Internal auditors should consider the following suggestions when planning engagements. This guidance is not intended to represent all the considerations that may be necessary, but simply a recommended set of items that should be addressed.

1. The internal auditor is responsible for planning and conducting the engagement assignment, subject to supervisory review and approval. The engagement program should:
    *   Document the internal auditor's procedures for collecting, analyzing, interpreting, and documenting information during the engagement.
    *   State the objectives of the engagement.
    *   Set forth the scope and degree of testing required to achieve the engagement objectives in each phase of the engagement.
    *   Identify technical aspects, activity objectives, risks, processes, and transactions that should be examined.
    *   State the nature and extent of testing required.
    *   Be prepared prior to the commencement of engagement work and modified, as appropriate, during the course of the engagement.

2. The chief audit executive is responsible for determining how, when, and to whom engagement results will be communicated. This determination should be documented and communicated to management, to the extent deemed practical, during the planning phase of the engagement. Subsequent changes, which affect the timing or reporting of engagement results, should also be communicated to management, if appropriate.

3. Other requirements of the engagement, such as the engagement period covered and estimated completion dates, should be determined. The final engagement communication format should be considered, since proper planning at this stage facilitates preparing the final engagement communication.

4. All those in management who need to know about the engagement should be informed. Meetings should be held with management responsible for the activity being examined. A summary of matters discussed at meetings and any conclusions reached should be prepared, distributed to individuals, as appropriate, and retained in the engagement working papers. Topics of discussion may include:
   - Planned engagement objectives and scope of work.
   - The timing of engagement work.
   - Internal auditors assigned to the engagement.
   - The process of communicating throughout the engagement, including the methods, time frames, and individuals who will be responsible.
   - Business conditions and operations of the activity being reviewed, including recent changes in management or major systems.
   - Concerns or any requests of management.
   - Matters of particular interest or concern to the internal auditor.
   - Description of the internal auditing activity's reporting procedures and follow-up process.

Practice Advisory 2210-1: Engagement Objectives

Interpretation of *Standard 2210* from the *International Standards for the Professional Practice of Internal Auditing*

Related Standard
2210 – Engagement Objectives
The internal audit activity should evaluate the design, implementation, and effectiveness of the organization's ethics-related objectives, programs, and activities.

Nature of this Practice Advisory: Internal auditors should consider the following suggestions when establishing engagement objectives. This guidance is not intended to represent all the considerations that may be necessary, but simply a recommended set of items that should be addressed.

1. Planning should be documented. Engagement objectives and scope of work should be established. Engagement objectives are broad statements developed by internal auditors and define what the engagement is intended to accomplish. Engagement procedures are the means to attain engagement objectives. Engagement objectives and procedures, taken together, define the scope of the internal auditor's work.

2. Engagement objectives and procedures should address the risks associated with the activity under review. The term risk is the uncertainty of an event occurring that could have an impact on the achievement of objectives. Risk is measured in terms of

consequences and likelihood. The purpose of the risk assessment during the planning phase of the engagement is to identify significant areas of activity that should be examined as potential engagement objectives.

Practice Advisory 2210.A1-1: Risk Assessment in Engagement Planning

**Interpretation of *Standard 2210.A1* from the
*International Standards for the
Professional Practice of Internal Auditing***

Related Standard
2210.A1 – Internal auditors should conduct a preliminary assessment of the risks relevant to the activity under review. Engagement objectives should reflect the results of this assessment.

Nature of this Practice Advisory: *Internal auditors should consider the following suggestions when assessing risk during engagement planning. This guidance is not intended to represent all the considerations that may be necessary during such an evaluation, but simply a recommended set of items that should be addressed. Internal auditors use their judgment to decide which items are needed to gain sufficient confidence that relevant risks are identified for a specific engagement.*

1. The internal auditor should consider management's assessment of risks relevant to the activity under review. The internal auditor will want to take into account:
   - The reliability of management's assessment of risk.
   - Management's monitoring and reporting of risk issues.
   - Management reports of events that have exceeded the agreed limits for risk toleration.

- Whether there are risks identified by management elsewhere in the organization in related activities or supporting systems that may be relevant to the activity under review.
- Management's own assessment of controls related to risks.

2. Background information should be obtained about the activities to be reviewed. A review of background information should be performed to determine the impact on the engagement. Relevant items may include:
   - Objectives and goals.
   - Policies, plans, procedures, laws, regulations, and contracts, which could have a significant impact on operations and reports.
   - Organizational information, e.g., number and names of employees, key employees, job descriptions, and details about recent changes in the organization, including major system changes.
   - Budget information, operating results, and financial data of the activity to be reviewed.
   - Prior engagement working papers.
   - Results of other engagements, including the work of external auditors, completed or in process.
   - Correspondence files to determine potential significant engagement issues.
   - Authoritative and technical literature appropriate to the activity.

3. If appropriate, a survey should be conducted to become familiar with the activities, risks, and controls, to identify areas for engagement emphasis, and to invite comments and suggestions from engagement clients. A survey is a process for gathering information, without detailed verification, on the activity being examined. The main purposes are to:
   - Understand the activity under review.
   - Identify significant areas warranting special emphasis.

- Obtain information for use in performing the engagement.
- Determine whether further auditing is necessary.

4. A survey permits an informed approach to planning and carrying out engagement work, and is an effective tool for applying the internal auditing activity's resources where they can be used most effectively. The focus of a survey will vary depending upon the nature of the engagement. The scope of work and the time requirements of a survey will vary. Contributing factors include the internal auditor's training and experience, knowledge of the activity being examined, the type of engagement being performed, and whether the survey is part of a recurring or follow-up assignment. Time requirements will also be influenced by the size and complexity of the activity being examined, and by the geographical dispersion of the activity.

5. A survey may involve use of the following procedures:
   - Discussions with the engagement client.
   - Interviews with individuals affected by the activity, e.g., users of the activity's output.
   - On-site observations.
   - Review of management reports and studies.
   - Analytical auditing procedures.
   - Flowcharting.
   - Functional "walk-through" (tests of specific work activities from beginning to end).
   - Documenting key control activities.

6. The internal auditor should prepare a summary of results from the reviews of management's assessment of risk, the background information, and findings from any survey work carried out. The summary should identify:
   - Significant engagement issues and reasons for pursuing them in more depth.
   - Pertinent information acquired from all sources.

- Engagement objectives, engagement procedures, and special approaches such as computer-assisted audit techniques.
- Potential critical control points, control deficiencies, and/or excess controls.
- Preliminary estimates of time and resource requirements.
- Revised dates for reporting phases and completing the engagement.
- When applicable, reasons for not continuing the engagement.

Practice Advisory 2230-1: Engagement Resource Allocation

Interpretation of *Standard 2230* from the
*International Standards for the
Professional Practice of Internal Auditing*

Related Standard
2230 – Engagement Resource Allocation
Internal auditors should determine appropriate resources to achieve engagement objectives. Staffing should be based on an evaluation of the nature and complexity of each engagement, time constraints, and available resources.

Nature of this Practice Advisory: Internal auditors should consider the following suggestions when determining engagement resource allocation. This guidance is not intended to represent all the considerations that may be necessary, but simply a recommended set of items that should be addressed.

In determining the resources necessary to perform the engagement, evaluation of the following is important:

- The number and experience level of the internal auditing staff required should be based on an evaluation of the nature and complexity of the engagement assignment, time constraints, and available resources.
- Knowledge, skills, and other competencies of the internal audit staff should be considered in selecting internal auditors for the engagement.

- Training needs of internal auditors should be considered, since each engagement assignment serves as a basis for meeting developmental needs of the internal auditing activity.
- Consideration of the use of external resources in instances where additional knowledge, skills, and other competencies are needed.

Practice Advisory 2240-1:
Engagement Work Program

Interpretation of *Standard 2240* from the
International Standards for the
Professional Practice of Internal Auditing

Related Standard
2240 – Engagement Work Program
Internal auditors should develop work programs that achieve the engagement objectives. These work programs should be recorded.

Nature of this Practice Advisory: Internal auditors should consider the following suggestions when developing engagement work programs. This guidance is not intended to represent all the considerations that may be necessary, but simply a recommended set of items that should be addressed.

1. Engagement procedures, including the testing and sampling techniques employed, should be selected in advance, where practicable, and expanded or altered if circumstances warrant. More detailed guidance is described in Practice Advisory 2210.A1-1.

2. The process of collecting, analyzing, interpreting, and documenting information should be supervised to provide reasonable assurance that the auditor's objectivity is maintained and engagement goals are met. More detailed guidance is described in Practice Advisory 2340-1.

Practice Advisory 2240.A1-1:
Approval of Work Programs

**Interpretation of *Standard 2240.A1* from the
*International Standards for the
Professional Practice of Internal Auditing***

> *Related Standard*
> **2240.A1** – Work programs should establish the procedures for identifying, analyzing, evaluating, and recording information during the engagement. The work program should be approved prior to the commencement of work, and any adjustments approved promptly.

Nature of this Practice Advisory: Internal auditors should consider the following suggestions when approving work programs. This guidance is not intended to represent all the considerations that may be necessary, but simply a recommended set of items that should be addressed.

1. In obtaining approval of the engagement work plan, such plans should be approved in writing by the chief audit executive or designee prior to the commencement of engagement work, where practicable. Initially, approval may be obtained orally, if factors preclude obtaining written approval prior to commencing engagement work. Adjustments to engagement work plans should be approved in a timely manner.

Practice Advisory 2300-1:
Internal Auditing's Use of
Personal Information in
Conducting Audits

**Interpretation of *Standard 2300* from the
*International Standards for the
Professional Practice of Internal Auditing***

Related Standard
2300 – Performing the Engagement
Internal auditors should identify, analyze, evaluate, and record
sufficient information to achieve the engagement's objectives.

---

*Nature of this Practice Advisory: Internal auditors should
consider the following suggestions when considering the use of
personal information in the conduct of an assurance or
consulting engagement. This practice advisory is not intended
as comprehensive guidance related to the use of personal
information, but rather a reminder of the importance of its
appropriate use in accordance with the laws and policies of the
relevant jurisdiction where the audit is being conducted and
where the organization conducts business.*

1. Concerns relating to the protection of personal privacy and
    information are becoming more apparent, focused, and global
    as advancements in information technology and communications
    continually introduce new risks and threats to privacy. Privacy
    controls are legal requirements for doing business in most of the
    world.

2. Personal information generally refers to information that can be associated with a specific individual, or that has identifying characteristics that might be combined with other information to do so.[2] It can include any factual or subjective information, recorded or not, in any form or media. Personal information might include, for example:

    - Name, address, identification numbers, income, or blood type;
    - Evaluations, comments, social status, or disciplinary actions; and
    - Employee files, credit records, loan records.

3. For the most part, laws require organizations to identify the purposes for which personal information is collected, at or before the time the information is collected; and that personal information not be used or disclosed for purposes other than those for which it was collected, except with the consent of the individual or as required by law.

4. It is important that the internal auditor understands and complies with all laws regarding the use of personal information in their jurisdiction and those jurisdictions where their organization conducts business.

5. The internal auditor must understand that it may be inappropriate, and in some cases illegal, to access, retrieve, review, manipulate, or use personal information in conducting certain internal audit engagements.

6. The internal auditor should investigate issues before initiating audit effort and seek advice from in-house legal counsel if there are any questions or concerns in this respect.

---

[2]Hargraves, Kim, Susan B. Lione, Kerry L. Shackleford, and Peter C. Tilton, *Privacy: Assessing the Risk* (Altamonte Springs, FL: The Institute of Internal Auditors Research Foundation, 2003).

Practice Advisory 2310-1:
Identifying Information

Interpretation of *Standard 2310* from the
*International Standards for the
Professional Practice of Internal Auditing*

Related Standard
2310 – Identifying Information
Internal auditors should identify sufficient, reliable, relevant, and
useful information to achieve the engagement's objectives.

---

*Nature of this Practice Advisory: Internal auditors should
consider the following suggestions when identifying information.
This guidance is not intended to represent all the considerations
that may be necessary, but simply a recommended set of items
that should be addressed.*

1. Information should be collected on all matters related to the
   engagement objectives and scope of work. Internal auditors use
   analytical auditing procedures when identifying and examining
   information. Analytical auditing procedures are performed by
   studying and comparing relationships among both financial and
   nonfinancial information. The application of analytical auditing
   procedures for identifying information to be examined is based
   on the premise that, in the absence of known conditions to the
   contrary, relationships among information may reasonably be
   expected to exist and continue. Examples of contrary conditions
   include unusual or nonrecurring transactions or events;
   accounting, organizational, operational, environmental, and

technological changes; inefficiencies; ineffectiveness; errors; irregularities; or illegal acts.

2. Information should be sufficient, competent, relevant, and useful to provide a sound basis for engagement observations and recommendations. Sufficient information is factual, adequate, and convincing so that a prudent, informed person would reach the same conclusions as the auditor. Competent information is reliable and the best attainable through the use of appropriate engagement techniques. Relevant information supports engagement observations and recommendations and is consistent with the objectives for the engagement. Useful information helps the organization meet its goals.

Practice Advisory 2320-1:
Analysis and Evaluation

Interpretation of *Standard 2320* from the
International Standards for the
Professional Practice of Internal Auditing

Related Standard
2320 – Analysis and Evaluation
Internal auditors should base conclusions and engagement results
on appropriate analyses and evaluations.

---

*Nature of this Practice Advisory: Internal auditors should
consider the following suggestions when using analysis and
evaluation to reach conclusions. This guidance is not intended
to represent all the considerations that may be necessary during
such an evaluation, but simply a recommended set of items that
should be addressed.*

1. Analytical audit procedures provide internal auditors with an
   efficient and effective means of assessing and evaluating
   information collected in an engagement. The assessment results
   from comparing information with expectations identified or
   developed by the internal auditor. Analytical audit procedures
   are useful in identifying, among other things:
   - Differences that are not expected.
   - The absence of differences when they are expected.
   - Potential errors.
   - Potential irregularities or illegal acts.
   - Other unusual or nonrecurring transactions or events.

2. Analytical audit procedures may include:
   - Comparison of current period information with similar information for prior periods.
   - Comparison of current period information with budgets or forecasts.
   - Study of relationships of financial information with the appropriate nonfinancial information (for example, recorded payroll expense compared to changes in average number of employees).
   - Study of relationships among elements of information (for example, fluctuation in recorded interest expense compared to changes in related debt balances).
   - Comparison of information with similar information for other organizational units.
   - Comparison of information with similar information for the industry in which the organization operates.

3. Analytical audit procedures may be performed using monetary amounts, physical quantities, ratios, or percentages. Specific analytical audit procedures include, but are not limited to, ratio, trend, and regression analysis, reasonableness tests, period-to-period comparisons, comparisons with budgets, forecasts, and external economic information. Analytical audit procedures assist internal auditors in identifying conditions which may require subsequent engagement procedures. Internal auditors should use analytical audit procedures in planning the engagement in accordance with the guidelines contained in Section 2200 of the *International Standards for the Professional Practice of Internal Auditing (Standards)* (Practice Advisory 2210-1).

4. Analytical audit procedures should also be used during the engagement to examine and evaluate information to support engagement results. Internal auditors should consider the factors listed below in determining the extent to which analytical audit procedures should be used. After evaluating these factors,

internal auditors should consider and use additional audit procedures, as necessary, to achieve the engagement objective.
- The significance of the area being examined
- The assessment of risk and effectiveness of risk management in the area being examined
- The adequacy of the system of internal control
- The availability and reliability of financial and nonfinancial information
- The precision with which the results of analytical audit procedures can be predicted
- The availability and comparability of information regarding the industry in which the organization operates
- The extent to which other engagement procedures provide support for engagement results

5. When analytical audit procedures identify unexpected results or relationships, internal auditors should examine and evaluate such results or relationships. This examination and evaluation should include making inquiries of management, and application of other engagement procedures until internal auditors are satisfied that the results or relationships are sufficiently explained. Unexplained results or relationships from applying analytical audit procedures may be indicative of a significant condition such as a potential error, irregularity, or illegal act. Results or relationships that are not sufficiently explained should be communicated to the appropriate levels of management. Internal auditors may recommend appropriate courses of action, depending on the circumstances.

Practice Advisory 2330-1: Recording Information

**Interpretation of *Standard 2330* from the
*International Standards for the
Professional Practice of Internal Auditing***

Related Standard
2330 – Recording Information
Internal auditors should record relevant information to support the conclusions and engagement results.

Nature of this Practice Advisory: Internal auditors should consider the following suggestions when recording information. This guidance is not intended to represent all the considerations that may be necessary, but simply a recommended set of items that should be addressed.

1. Working papers that document the engagement should be prepared by the internal auditor and reviewed by management of the internal audit activity. The working papers should record the information obtained and the analyses made and should support the bases for the observations and recommendations to be reported. Engagement working papers generally:
   - Provide the principal support for the engagement communications.
   - Aid in the planning, performance, and review of engagements.
   - Document whether the engagement objectives were achieved.
   - Facilitate third-party reviews.

- Provide a basis for evaluating the internal audit activity's quality program.
- Provide support in circumstances such as insurance claims, fraud cases, and lawsuits.
- Aid in the professional development of the internal audit staff.
- Demonstrate the internal audit activity's compliance with the *International Standards for the Professional Practice of Internal Auditing (Standards)*.

2. The organization, design, and content of engagement working papers will depend on the nature of the engagement. Engagement working papers should document the following aspects of the engagement process:
   - Planning
   - Risk assessment
   - The examination and evaluation of the adequacy and effectiveness of the system of internal control
   - The engagement procedures performed, the information obtained, and the conclusions reached
   - Review
   - Communication
   - Follow-up

3. Engagement working papers should be complete and include support for engagement conclusions reached. Among other things, engagement working papers may include:
   - Planning documents and engagement programs.
   - Control questionnaires, flowcharts, checklists, and narratives.
   - Notes and memoranda resulting from interviews.
   - Organizational data, such as organization charts and job descriptions.
   - Copies of important contracts and agreements.
   - Information about operating and financial policies.

- Results of control evaluations.
- Letters of confirmation and representation.
- Analysis and tests of transactions, processes, and account balances.
- Results of analytical auditing procedures.
- The engagement's final communications and management's responses.
- Engagement correspondence if it documents engagement conclusions reached.

4. Engagement working papers may be in the form of paper, tapes, disks, diskettes, films, or other media. If engagement working papers are in the form of media other than paper, consideration should be given to generating backup copies.

5. If internal auditors are reporting on financial information, the engagement working papers should document whether the accounting records agree or reconcile with such financial information.

6. The chief audit executive should establish working paper policies for the various types of engagements performed. Standardized engagement working papers such as questionnaires and audit programs may improve the efficiency of an engagement and facilitate the delegation of engagement work. Some engagement working papers may be categorized as permanent or carry-forward engagement files. These files generally contain information of continuing importance.

7. The following are typical engagement working paper preparation techniques:
    - Each engagement working paper should identify the engagement and describe the contents or purpose of the working paper.

- Each engagement working paper should be signed (or initialed) and dated by the internal auditor performing the work.
- Each engagement working paper should contain an index or reference number.
- Audit verification symbols (tick marks) should be explained.
- Sources of data should be clearly identified.

Practice Advisory 2330.A1-1:
Control of Engagement Records

Interpretation of *Standard 2330.A1* from the
International Standards for the
Professional Practice of Internal Auditing

> *Related Standard*
> **2330.A1** – The chief audit executive should control access to engagement records. The chief audit executive should obtain the approval of senior management and/or legal counsel prior to releasing such records to external parties, as appropriate.

Nature of this Practice Advisory: Internal auditors should consider the following suggestions involving control of engagement records. This guidance is not intended to represent all the considerations that may be necessary, but simply a recommended set of items that should be addressed.

1. Engagement working papers are the property of the organization. Engagement working paper files should generally remain under the control of the internal audit activity and should be accessible only to authorized personnel.

2. Management and other members of the organization may request access to engagement working papers. Such access may be necessary to substantiate or explain engagement observations and recommendations or to utilize engagement documentation for other business purposes. These requests for access should be subject to the approval of the chief audit executive (CAE).

3. It is common practice for internal and external auditors to grant access to each other's audit working papers. Access to audit working papers by external auditors should be subject to the approval of the CAE.

4. There are circumstances where parties outside the organization, other than external auditors, request access to audit working papers and reports. Prior to releasing such documentation, the CAE should obtain the approval of senior management and/or legal counsel, as appropriate.

Practice Advisory 2330.A1-2:
Legal Considerations in
Granting Access to Engagement Records

Interpretation of *Standard 2330.A1* from the
International Standards for the
Professional Practice of Internal Auditing

Related Standard
2330.A1 – Recording Information
The chief audit executive should control access to engagement records. The chief audit executive should obtain approval of senior management and/or legal counsel prior to releasing such records to external parties.

Nature of this Practice Advisory: Internal auditors should consider the following suggestions when considering granting access to engagement records to those outside the internal audit activity. This guidance is not intended to represent all the considerations that may be necessary.

Caution — *Internal auditors are encouraged to consult legal counsel in all matters involving legal issues as requirements may vary significantly in different jurisdictions. The guidance contained in this Practice Advisory is based primarily on the legal system in the United States of America.*

1. Internal audit engagement records include reports, supporting documentation, review notes, and correspondence, regardless of storage media. Internal auditors, with the support of management and governing boards to whom they provide audit

services, develop the engagement records. Engagement records are generally produced under the presumption that their contents are confidential and may contain a mix of both facts and opinions. However, those who are not immediately familiar with the organization or its internal audit process may misunderstand these facts and opinions. Access to engagement records by outside parties has been sought in several different types of proceedings, including criminal prosecutions, civil litigation, tax audits, regulatory reviews, government contract reviews, and reviews by self-regulatory organizations. Virtually all of an organization's records that are not protected by the attorney-client privilege are accessible in criminal proceedings. In noncriminal proceedings the issue of access is less clear and may vary according to the legal jurisdiction of the organization.

2. Explicit practices in the following documents of the internal audit activity may increase the control of access to engagement records. These suggestions are discussed in the paragraphs below:
    - Charter
    - Job descriptions
    - Internal department policies
    - Procedures for handling investigations with legal counsel

3. The internal audit charter should address access to and control of organizational records and information, regardless of media used to store the records.

4. Written job descriptions should be created for the internal audit activity and should include the complex and varied duties auditors perform. Such descriptions may help internal auditors when addressing requests for engagement records. They will also help internal auditors understand the scope of their work and external parties to comprehend the duties of internal auditors.

5. Internal department policies should be developed with regard to the operation of the internal audit activity. These written practices should cover, among other matters, what should be included in engagement records, how long departmental records should be retained, how outside requests for access to department records should be handled, and what special practices should be followed in handling an investigation with legal counsel. These are discussed below.

6. A policy relating to the various types of engagements should specify the content and format of the engagement records and how internal auditors should handle their review notes, i.e., retained as a record of issues raised and subsequently resolved or destroyed so third parties cannot gain access to them. Also, a policy should specify the length of retention for engagement records. These time limits will be determined by the needs of the organization as well as legal requirements. (It is important to check with legal counsel on this issue.)

7. Departmental policies should explain who in the organization is responsible for ensuring the control and security of departmental records, who can be granted access to engagement records, and how requests for access to those records are to be handled. These policies may depend on the practices followed in the industry or legal jurisdiction of the organization. The chief audit executive and others in internal auditing should be alert to changing practices in the industry and changing legal precedents. They should anticipate those who might someday seek access to their work products.

8. The policy granting access to engagement records should also address the following issues:
    *   Process for resolving access issues;
    *   Time period for retention of each type of work product;

- Process for educating and reeducating the internal audit staff concerning the risks and issues regarding access to their work products; and
- Requirement for periodically surveying the industry to determine who may want access to the work product in the future.

9. A policy should provide guidance to the internal auditor in determining when an audit warrants an investigation, that is, when an audit becomes an investigation to be handled with an attorney and what special procedures should be followed in communicating with the legal counsel. The policy should also cover the matter of executing a proper retention letter to have any information given to the attorney be privileged.

10. Internal auditors should also educate the board and management about the risks of access to engagement records. The policies relating to who can be granted access to engagement records, how those requests are to be handled, and what procedures are to be followed when an audit warrants an investigation should be reviewed by the audit committee of the board of directors (or equivalent governing body). The specific policies will vary depending upon the nature of the organization and the access privileges that have been established by law.

11. Careful preparation of engagement records is important when disclosure is required. The following steps should be considered:
    - Only disclose the specific documents requested. Engagement records with opinions and recommendations are generally not released. Documents that reveal attorneys' thought processes or strategies will usually be privileged and not subject to forced disclosure.
    - Only release copies, keeping the originals, especially if the documents were prepared in pencil. If the court requests originals, the internal audit activity should keep a copy.

- Label each document as confidential and place a notation on each document that secondary distribution is not permitted without permission.

Practice Advisory 2330.A2-1: Retention of Records

**Interpretation of *Standard 2330.A2* from the
*International Standards for the
Professional Practice of Internal Auditing***

> ***Related Standard***
> **2330.A2** – The chief audit executive should develop retention requirements for engagement records. These retention requirements should be consistent with the organization's guidelines and any pertinent regulatory or other requirements.

Nature of this Practice Advisory: *Internal auditors should consider the following suggestions when developing record retention requirements. This guidance is not intended to represent all the considerations that may be necessary, but simply a recommended set of items that should be addressed.*

1. Record retention requirements should be designed to include all engagement records, regardless of the format in which the records are stored.

Practice Advisory 2340-1:
Engagement Supervision

Interpretation of *Standard 2340* from the
International Standards for the
Professional Practice of Internal Auditing

Related Standard
2340 – Engagement Supervision
Engagements should be properly supervised to ensure objectives
are achieved, quality is assured, and staff is developed.

Nature of this Practice Advisory: Internal auditors should
consider the following suggestions when supervising
engagements. This guidance is not intended to represent all the
considerations that may be necessary, but simply a recommended
set of items that should be addressed.

1. The chief audit executive (CAE) is responsible for assuring that
    appropriate engagement supervision is provided. Supervision is
    a process that begins with planning and continues throughout
    the examination, evaluation, communication, and follow-up phases
    of the engagement. Supervision includes:
    *   Ensuring that the auditors assigned possess the requisite
        knowledge, skills, and other competencies to perform the
        engagement.
    *   Providing appropriate instructions during the planning of the
        engagement and approving the engagement program.
    *   Seeing that the approved engagement program is carried
        out unless changes are both justified and authorized.

- Determining that engagement working papers adequately support the engagement observations, conclusions, and recommendations.
- Ensuring that engagement communications are accurate, objective, clear, concise, constructive, and timely.
- Ensuring that engagement objectives are met.
- Providing opportunities for developing internal auditors' knowledge, skills, and other competencies.

2. Appropriate evidence of supervision should be documented and retained. The extent of supervision required will depend on the proficiency and experience of internal auditors and the complexity of the engagement. The CAE has overall responsibility for review but may designate appropriately experienced members of the internal audit activity to perform the review. Appropriately experienced internal auditors may be utilized to review the work of other less experienced internal auditors.

3. All internal audit assignments, whether performed by or for the internal audit activity, remain the responsibility of the CAE. The CAE is responsible for all significant professional judgments made in the planning, examination, evaluation, report, and follow-up phases of the engagement. The CAE should adopt suitable means to ensure that this responsibility is met. Suitable means include policies and procedures designed to:
   - Minimize the risk that professional judgments may be made by internal auditors or others performing work for the internal audit activity that are inconsistent with the professional judgment of the CAE such that a significant adverse effect on the engagement could result.
   - Resolve differences in professional judgment between the CAE and internal audit staff members over significant issues relating to the engagement. Such means may include: (a) discussion of pertinent facts; (b) further inquiry and/or research; and (c) documentation and disposition of the

differing viewpoints in the engagement working papers. In instances of a difference in professional judgment over an ethical issue, suitable means may include referral of the issue to those individuals in the organization having responsibility over ethical matters.

4. Supervision extends to staff training and development, employee performance evaluation, time and expense control, and similar administrative areas.

5. All engagement working papers should be reviewed to ensure that they properly support the engagement communications and that all necessary audit procedures have been performed. Evidence of supervisory review should consist of the reviewer initialing and dating each working paper after it is reviewed. Other techniques that provide evidence of supervisory review include completing an engagement working paper review checklist, preparing a memorandum specifying the nature, extent, and results of the review, and/or evaluation and acceptance within electronic working paper software.

6. Reviewers may make a written record (review notes) of questions arising from the review process. When clearing review notes, care should be taken to ensure that the working papers provide adequate evidence that questions raised during the review have been resolved. Acceptable alternatives with respect to disposition of review notes are as follows:
   - Retain the review notes as a record of the questions raised by the reviewer and the steps taken in their resolution.
   - Discard the review notes after the questions raised have been resolved and the appropriate engagement working papers have been amended to provide the additional information requested.

Practice Advisory 2400-1:
Legal Considerations in
Communicating Results

Interpretation of *Standard 2100* from the
International Standards for the
Professional Practice of Internal Auditing

Related Standard
2400 – Communicating Results
Internal auditors should communicate the engagement results.

Nature of this Practice Advisory: Internal auditors should consider the following suggestions when communicating the results of audit engagements. This guidance is not intended to represent all the considerations that may be necessary when communicating results.

Caution – *Internal auditors are encouraged to consult legal counsel in all matters involving legal issues as requirements may vary significantly in different jurisdictions. The guidance contained in this Practice Advisory is based primarily on the United States' legal system.*

1. Internal auditors should exercise caution when including results and issuing opinions in audit communications and work papers regarding law and regulatory violations and other legal issues. Established policies and procedures regarding the handling of these matters and a close working relationship with other appropriate areas (legal counsel, compliance, etc.) is strongly encouraged.

2. Internal auditors are required to gather evidence, make analytical judgments, report their results, and ensure corrective action is taken. Internal auditors' requirement for documenting engagement records may conflict with legal counsel's desire not to leave discoverable evidence that could harm a defense. For example, even if an internal auditor conducts an investigation properly, the facts disclosed may harm the organization counsel's case. Proper planning and policy making is essential so that a sudden revelation does not place the corporate counsel and internal auditor at odds with one another. These policies should include role definition and methods of communication. The internal auditor and corporate counsel should also foster an ethical and preventive perspective throughout the organization by sensitizing and educating management about the established policies. Internal auditors should consider the following, especially in connection with engagements that may give rise to disclosing or communicating results to parties outside the organization.

3. There are four elements necessary to protect the attorney-client privilege. There must be:
    *   A communication;
    *   Made between "privileged persons";
    *   In confidence; and
    *   For the purpose of seeking, obtaining, or providing legal assistance for the client.
    This privilege, which is used primarily to protect communications with attorneys, can also apply to communications with third parties working with the attorney.

4. Some courts have recognized a privilege of critical self-analysis that shields from discovery self-critical materials like audit work product. In general, the recognition of this privilege is premised on the belief that the confidentiality of the reviews in the instances involved outweighs the valued public interests. As one court explained:

The self-critical analysis privilege has been recognized as a qualified privilege that protects from discovery certain critical self-appraisals. It allows individuals or businesses to candidly assess their compliance with regulatory and legal requirements without creating evidence that may be used against them by their opponents in future litigation. The rationale for the doctrine is that such critical self-evaluation fosters the compelling public interest in observance of the law.

5. In general, three requirements must usually be met for the privilege to apply:
    - The information subject to the privilege must result from a self-critical analysis undertaken by the party asserting the privilege;
    - The public must have a strong interest in preserving the free flow of the information contained in the critical analysis;
    - The information must be of the type whose flow would be curtailed if discovery were allowed.

    In some instances, courts also have considered whether the critical analysis preceded or caused the plaintiff's injury, where the analysis comes after the events giving rise to the claim, the justification for the privilege is said to be at its strongest.

6. The courts have been generally more reluctant to recognize self-evaluative privileges when the documents are sought by a government agency rather than a private litigant; presumably this reluctance results from recognition of the government's relatively stronger interest in enforcing the law. The self-evaluative privilege is particularly relevant to functions and activities that have established self-regulatory procedures. Hospitals, security brokers, and public accounting firms are among those that have established such procedures. Most of these procedures are associated with quality assurance procedures that have been added to an operating activity such as financial auditing.

7. There are three elements that must be satisfied to protect documents from disclosure under the work-product doctrine. Documents must be:
   - Some type of work product (i.e., memo, computer program);
   - Prepared in anticipation of litigation; and
   - The party preparing must be an agent of the attorney.

8. Documents prepared before the attorney-client relationship comes into existence are not protected by the work-product doctrine. Delivering documents, prepared before the attorney-client relationship is formed, to the attorney will not protect those documents under the work-product doctrine. In addition, the doctrine is qualified. The documents will not be protected under the doctrine if a substantial need for the information exists and the information is not otherwise available without undue hardship. Thus in Re: *Grand Jury*, the audit committee of the corporation conducted interviews to determine if any questionable foreign payments were made. Their report was protected from discovery under the work-product doctrine except for those portions that contained the results of the interviews with deceased persons. (599 F.2d 1224 (1979)).

Practice Advisory 2410-1:
Communication Criteria

**Interpretation of *Standard 2410* from the
*International Standards for the
Professional Practice of Internal Auditing***

Related Standard
2410 – Criteria for Communicating
Communications should include the engagement's objectives and scope as well as applicable conclusions, recommendations, and action plans.

Related Standard
2410.A1 – The final communication of results should, where appropriate, contain the internal auditor's overall opinion or conclusions.

Nature of this Practice Advisory: Internal auditors should consider the following suggestions when communicating the results of engagements. This guidance is not intended to represent all the considerations that may be necessary, but simply a recommended set of items that should be addressed.

1. Although the format and content of the engagement final communications may vary by organization or type of engagement, they should contain, at a minimum, the purpose, scope, and results of the engagement.

2. Engagement final communications may include background information and summaries. Background information may

identify the organizational units and activities reviewed and provide relevant explanatory information. It may also include the status of observations, conclusions, and recommendations from prior reports and an indication of whether the report covers a scheduled engagement or is responding to a request. Summaries, if included, should be balanced representations of the engagement communication's content.

3. Purpose statements should describe the engagement objectives and may, where necessary, inform the reader why the engagement was conducted and what it was expected to achieve.

4. Scope statements should identify the audited activities and include, where appropriate, supportive information such as time period reviewed. Related activities not reviewed should be identified if necessary to delineate the boundaries of the engagement. The nature and extent of engagement work performed also should be described.

5. Results should include observations, conclusions, opinions, recommendations, and action plans.

6. Observations are pertinent statements of fact. Those observations necessary to support or prevent misunderstanding of the internal auditor's conclusions and recommendations should be included in the final engagement communications. Less significant observations or recommendations may be communicated informally.

7. Engagement observations and recommendations emerge by a process of comparing what should be with what is. Whether or not there is a difference, the internal auditor has a foundation on which to build the report. When conditions meet the criteria, acknowledgment in the engagement communications of

satisfactory performance may be appropriate. Observations and recommendations should be based on the following attributes:

- Criteria: The standards, measures, or expectations used in making an evaluation and/or verification (what should exist).
- Condition: The factual evidence that the internal auditor found in the course of the examination (what does exist).
- Cause: The reason for the difference between the expected and actual conditions (why the difference exists).
- Effect: The risk or exposure the organization and/or others encounter because the condition is not consistent with the criteria (the impact of the difference). In determining the degree of risk or exposure, internal auditors should consider the effect their engagement observations and recommendations may have on the organization's operations and financial statements.
- Observations and recommendations may also include engagement client accomplishments, related issues, and supportive information, if not included elsewhere.

8. Conclusions and opinions are the internal auditor's evaluations of the effects of the observations and recommendations on the activities reviewed. They usually put the observations and recommendations in perspective based upon their overall implications. Engagement conclusions, if included in the engagement report, should be clearly identified as such. Conclusions may encompass the entire scope of an engagement or specific aspects. They may cover, but are not limited to, whether operating or program objectives and goals conform with those of the organization, whether the organization's objectives and goals are being met, and whether the activity under review is functioning as intended. An opinion may include an overall assessment of controls or area under review or may be limited to specific controls or aspects of the engagement.

9. Engagement communications should include recommendations for potential improvements, acknowledgments of satisfactory performance, and corrective actions. Recommendations are based on the internal auditor's observations and conclusions. They call for action to correct existing conditions or improve operations. Recommendations may suggest approaches to correcting or enhancing performance as a guide for management in achieving desired results. Recommendations may be general or specific. For example, under some circumstances, it may be desirable to recommend a general course of action and specific suggestions for implementation. In other circumstances, it may be appropriate only to suggest further investigation or study.

10. Engagement client accomplishments, in terms of improvements since the last engagement or the establishment of a well-controlled operation, may be included in the engagement final communications. This information may be necessary to fairly present the existing conditions and to provide a proper perspective and appropriate balance to the engagement final communications.

11. The engagement client's views about engagement conclusions, opinions, or recommendations may be included in the engagement communications.

12. As part of the internal auditor's discussions with the engagement client, the internal auditor should try to obtain agreement on the results of the engagement and on a plan of action to improve operations, as needed. If the internal auditor and engagement client disagree about the engagement results, the engagement communications may state both positions and the reasons for the disagreement. The engagement client's written comments may be included as an appendix to the engagement report. Alternatively, the engagement client's views may be presented in the body of the report or in a cover letter.

13. Certain information may not be appropriate for disclosure to all report recipients because it is privileged, proprietary, or related to improper or illegal acts. Such information, however, may be disclosed in a separate report. If the conditions being reported involve senior management, report distribution should be to the board of the organization.

14. Interim reports may be written or oral and may be transmitted formally or informally. Interim reports may be used to communicate information that requires immediate attention, to communicate a change in engagement scope for the activity under review, or to keep management informed of engagement progress when engagements extend over a long period. The use of interim reports does not diminish or eliminate the need for a final report.

15. A signed report should be issued after the engagement is completed. Summary reports highlighting engagement results may be appropriate for levels of management above the engagement client. They may be issued separately from or in conjunction with the final report. The term signed means that the authorized internal auditor's name should be manually signed in the report. Alternatively, the signature may appear on a cover letter. The internal auditor authorized to sign the report should be designated by the chief audit executive. If engagement reports are distributed by electronic means, a signed version of the report should be kept on file by the internal audit activity.

Practice Advisory 2420-1: Quality of Communications

**Interpretation of *Standard 2420* from the
*International Standards for the
Professional Practice of Internal Auditing***

Related Standard
2420 – Quality of Communications
Communications should be accurate, objective, clear, concise, constructive, complete, and timely.

Nature of this Practice Advisory: Internal auditors should consider the following suggestions when preparing communications. This guidance is not intended to represent all the considerations that may be necessary, but simply a recommended set of items that should be addressed.

1. Accurate communications are free from errors and distortions and are faithful to the underlying facts. The manner in which the data and evidence are gathered, evaluated, and summarized for presentation should be done with care and precision.

2. Objective communications are fair, impartial, and unbiased and are the result of a fair-minded and balanced assessment of all relevant facts and circumstances. Observations, conclusions, and recommendations should be derived and expressed without prejudice, partisanship, personal interests, and the undue influence of others.

3. Clear communications are easily understood and logical. Clarity can be improved by avoiding unnecessary technical language and providing all significant and relevant information.

4. Concise communications are to the point and avoid unnecessary elaboration, superfluous detail, redundancy, and wordiness. They are created by a persistent practice of revising and editing a presentation. The goal is that each thought will be meaningful but succinct.

5. Constructive communications are helpful to the engagement client and the organization and lead to improvements where needed. The contents and tone of the presentation should be useful, positive, and well meaning and contribute to the objectives of the organization.

6. Complete communications are lacking nothing that is essential to the target audience and include all significant and relevant information and observations to support recommendations and conclusions.

7. Timely communications are well timed, opportune, and expedient for careful consideration by those who may act on the recommendations. The timing of the presentation of engagement results should be set without undue delay and with a degree of urgency so as to enable prompt, effective action.

Practice Advisory 2440-1:
Recipients of Engagement Results

Interpretation of *Standard 2440* from the
International Standards for the
Professional Practice of Internal Auditing

Related Standard
2440 – Recipients of Engagement Results
The chief audit executive should communicate results to the appropriate parties.

Related Standard
2440.A1 – The chief audit executive is responsible for communicating the final results to parties who can ensure that the results are given due consideration.

Nature of this Practice Advisory: Internal auditors should consider the following suggestions when reporting results. This guidance is not intended to represent all the considerations that may be necessary, but simply a recommended set of items that should be addressed.

1. Internal auditors should discuss conclusions and recommendations with appropriate levels of management before issuing final engagement communications.

2. Discussion of conclusions and recommendations is usually accomplished during the course of the engagement and/or at post-engagement meetings (exit interviews). Another technique is the review of draft engagement issues, observations, and

recommendations by management of the audited activity. These discussions and reviews help ensure that there have been no misunderstandings or misinterpretations of fact by providing the opportunity for the engagement client to clarify specific items and to express views of the observations, conclusions, and recommendations.

3. Although the level of participants in the discussions and reviews may vary by organization and by the nature of the report, they will generally include those individuals who are knowledgeable of detailed operations and those who can authorize the implementation of corrective action.

4. The chief audit executive (CAE) or designee should review and approve the final engagement communication before issuance and should decide to whom the report will be distributed. The CAE or a designee should approve and may sign all final reports. If specific circumstances warrant, consideration should be given to having the auditor-in-charge, supervisor, or lead auditor sign the report as a representative of the CAE.

5. Final engagement communication should be distributed to those members of the organization who are able to ensure that engagement results are given due consideration. This means that the report should go to those who are in a position to take corrective action or ensure that corrective action is taken. The final engagement communication should be distributed to management of the activity under review. Higher-level members in the organization may receive only a summary communication. Communications may also be distributed to other interested or affected parties such as external auditors and the board.

Practice Advisory 2440-2: Communications Outside the Organization

Interpretation of *Standard 2440* from the *International Standards for the Professional Practice of Internal Auditing*

Related Standard
2440 – Recipients of Engagement Results
The chief audit executive should communicate results to the appropriate parties.

Related Standard
2440.A2
If not otherwise mandated by legal, statutory, or regulatory requirements, prior to releasing results to parties outside the organization, the chief audit executive should:
- Assess the potential risk to the organization.
- Consult with senior management and/or legal counsel as appropriate.
- Control dissemination by restricting the use of the results.

Nature of this Practice Advisory: Internal auditors should consider the following guidance if called upon to disseminate information outside the organization. Such situations can arise when internal auditors are requested to provide a report or other information to someone outside the organization for which the internal audit services were provided. This guidance is a recommended set of items to be addressed and is not intended to represent all the considerations that may be necessary.

1. Internal auditors should review guidance contained in the engagement agreement or organizational policies and procedures related to reporting information outside the organization. The audit activity charter and the audit committee charter may also contain guidance related to reporting information outside the organization. If such guidance does not exist, the internal auditor should facilitate adoption of appropriate policies by the organization. Examples of information that could be included in the policies are:

    *   Authorization required to report information outside the organization.
    *   Process for seeking approval to report information outside the organization.
    *   Guidelines for permissible and non-permissible types of information that can be reported.
    *   Outside persons authorized to receive information and the types of information they can receive.
    *   Related privacy regulations, regulatory requirements, and legal considerations for reporting information outside the organization.
    *   Nature of assurances, advice, recommendations, opinions, guidance, and other information that can be included in communications resulting in dissemination of information outside the organization.

2. Requests can relate to information that already exists; for example, a previously issued internal audit report. Requests can also be received for information that must be created or determined, resulting in a new internal audit engagement. If the request relates to information or a report that already exists, the internal auditor should review the information to determine whether it is suitable for dissemination outside the organization.

3. In certain situations it may be possible to revise an existing report or information to make it suitable for dissemination outside the

organization. In other situations it may be possible to generate a new report based on work previously conducted. Appropriate due professional care should be exercised when revising, customizing, or creating a new report based on work previously conducted.

4. When reporting information outside the organization, the following matters should be considered:
    - Need for a written agreement concerning the information to be reported.
    - Identification of information providers, sources, report signers, information recipients, and related persons to the report or information disseminated.
    - Identification of objectives, scope, and procedures to be performed in generating applicable information.
    - Nature of report or other communication, including opinions, inclusion or exclusion of recommendations, disclaimers, limitations, and type of assurance or assertions to be provided.
    - Copyright issues and limitations on further distribution or sharing of the information.

5. Engagements performed to generate internal audit reports or communications to be reported outside the organization should be conducted in accordance with applicable *International Standards for the Professional Practice of Internal Auditing (Standards)* and include reference to such *Standards* in the report or other communication.

6. If during the conduct of engagements to disseminate information outside the organization the internal auditor discovers information deemed to be reportable to management or the audit committee, the internal auditor should provide suitable communication to appropriate individuals.

Practice Advisory 2440-3: Communicating Sensitive Information Within and Outside the Chain of Command

**Interpretation of *Standard 2440* and *Standard 2600*
from the
*International Standards for the
Professional Practice of Internal Auditing*
and Rules of Conduct in the
Code of Ethics for Integrity and Confidentiality**

Related Standard
2440 – Recipients of Engagement Results
The chief audit executive should report results to the appropriate individuals.

Related Standard
2600 – Resolution of Management's Acceptance of Risks
When the chief audit executive believes that senior management has accepted a level of residual risk that may be unacceptable to the organization, the chief audit executive should discuss the matter with senior management. If the decision regarding residual risk is not resolved, the chief audit executive and senior management should report the matter to the board for resolution.

> *Related Rules of Conduct of the Code of Ethics – Integrity*
> Internal auditors:
> 1.1 Shall perform their work with honesty, diligence, and responsibility.
> 1.2 Shall observe the law and make disclosures expected by the law and the profession.
> 1.3 Shall not knowingly be a party to any illegal activity, or engage in acts that are discreditable to the profession of internal auditing or to the organization.
> 1.4 Shall respect and contribute to the legitimate and ethical objectives of the organization.
>
> *Related Rules of Conduct of the Code of Ethics – Confidentiality*
> Internal auditors:
> 3.1 Shall be prudent in the use and protection of information acquired in the course of their duties.
> 3.2 Shall not use information for personal gain or in any manner that would be contrary to the law or detrimental to the legitimate and ethical objectives of the organization.

Nature of this Practice Advisory: An internal auditor may discover information about exposures, threats, uncertainties, fraud, waste and mismanagement, illegal activities, abuse of power, misconduct that endangers public health or safety, or other wrongdoings. In some cases, the new information will have significant consequences, and the supporting evidence will be substantial and credible. The internal auditor's dilemma that is posed in these types of situations is complex, often involving cultural and business practice differences, legal structures, local and national laws, as well as professional standards, ethical codes, and personal values. The manner in which the internal auditor seeks to resolve the situation may create reprisals and potential liability. Because of those risks and ramifications, the internal auditor should proceed with care to evaluate the evidence and the reasonableness of his or her conclusions and to examine the various potential actions that could be taken to communicate the sensitive information to persons who have the authority to resolve the matter and to stop the improper activity. In some countries, certain actions may be prescribed by local laws or regulations.

This Practice Advisory is offered to stimulate thinking about the many issues and challenges that the internal auditor may face in these situations. While providing information and suggesting factors that may be considered by an internal auditor, the Practice Advisory is not a comprehensive examination of the topic, and it does not offer legal or expert advice for the auditor. Internal auditors should seek legal counsel when the situation is sensitive and has significant consequences. This Practice Advisory was developed with the utmost care and after lengthy deliberation. However, The IIA does not assume responsibility for the use of the information contained in this Practice Advisory or for its applicability to specific situations in practice, and it does not give assurance that the suggested actions will be successful.

1. Internal auditors often come into the possession of information that is critically sensitive and substantial to the organization and has significant potential consequences. That information may relate to exposures, threats, uncertainties, fraud, waste and mismanagement, illegal activities, abuse of power, misconduct that endangers public health or safety, or other wrongdoings. Those types of matters may adversely impact the organization's reputation, image, competitiveness, success, viability, market values, investments and intangible assets, or earnings. They are likely to increase an organization's risk exposures.

Communicating Sensitive Information to Those in the Chain of Command

2. Once the internal auditor has decided that the new information is substantial and credible, the auditor would normally communicate the information, on a timely basis, to those in management who can act on it. In most instances, those communications will resolve the matter from an internal audit perspective, so long as management takes the appropriate action to manage the associated risks. If the communications result in a conclusion that management, by its inadequate or lack of actions, is exposing the organization to an unacceptable level of risk, the chief audit executive (CAE) should consider other options to achieve a satisfactory resolution.

3. Among those possible actions, the CAE could discuss his or her concerns about the risk exposure with senior management within his or her normal chain of command. Since the audit or other committee of the governing board would also be expected to be in the CAE's chain of command, the members of the board committee would normally be apprised of the CAE's concerns. If the CAE, after those discussions with senior management, is still unsatisfied and concludes that senior management is exposing the organization to an unacceptable risk and is not taking appropriate action to halt or correct the situation, senior management and the CAE would present the essential information and their differences of opinion to the members or a committee of the governing board.

4. That simple chain-of-command communication scenario may be accelerated for certain types of sensitive occurrences because of national laws, regulations, or commonly followed practices. For instance, in the case of evidence of fraudulent financial reporting by a company with publicly traded securities in the United States of America, regulations prescribe that the audit

committee of the board be immediately informed of the circumstances surrounding the possibility of misleading financial reports, even though senior management and the CAE may be in substantial agreement on what actions need to be taken. Laws and regulations in several countries specify that members or a committee of the governing board should be informed of discoveries of violations of criminal, securities, food, drugs, or pollution laws and other illegal acts, such as bribery or other improper payments to government officials or to agents of suppliers or customers.

Communicating Outside the Chain of Command

5. In some situations, an internal auditor may face the dilemma of considering whether to communicate the discovered information to persons outside the normal chain of command or even outside the organization. The act of disclosing adverse information to someone in the organization who is outside the individual's normal chain of command, or to a governmental agency or other authority that is wholly outside the organization, is commonly referred to as "whistleblowing."

6. In studies about whistleblowing, it has been reported that most whistleblowers disclose the sensitive information internally, even if outside the normal chain of command, particularly if they trust the policies and mechanisms of the organization to investigate an allegation of an illegal or other improper activity and to take appropriate action. However, some persons possessing sensitive information may decide to take the information outside the organization, particularly if they fear retribution by their employers or fellow employees, have doubt that the issue will be properly investigated, believe that it will be concealed, or possess evidence about an illegal or improper activity that jeopardizes the health, safety, or well-being of people in the organization or community.

The primary motive of most whistleblowers, who are acting on good faith, is to halt the illegal, harmful, or improper behavior.

7. An internal auditor who is facing a similar dilemma and needing to consider all possible options will need to evaluate alternative ways to communicate the risk to some person or group who is outside his or her normal chain of command. Because of risks and ramifications associated with these approaches, the internal auditor should proceed with care to evaluate the evidence and the reasonableness of his or her conclusions and to examine the merits and disadvantages of each potential action. Taking this type of action by an internal auditor may be appropriate if it will result in responsible action by persons in senior management or in governance positions, such as members of the governing board or one of its committees. An internal auditor would likely consider as his or her last option that of communicating outside the organization's governance structure. An internal auditor would reserve this type of action for those rare occasions when he or she is convinced that the risk and its possible consequences are serious and there is high probability that the organization's existing management and governance mechanisms cannot or will not effectively address the risk.

8. Many member countries in the OECD (Organization for Economic Cooperation and Development) have laws or administrative regulations requiring public servants with knowledge of illegal or unethical acts to inform an inspector general, other public official, or ombudsman. Some national laws pertaining to whistleblowing-type actions protect citizens if they come forward to disclose specific types of improper activities. Among the activities listed in the laws and regulations of those countries are:
   - Criminal offenses and other failures to comply with legal obligations.
   - Acts that are considered miscarriages of justice.

- Acts that endanger the health, safety, or well-being of individuals.
- Acts that damage the environment.
- Activities that conceal or cover up any of the above.

Other countries offer no guidance or protection. The internal auditor should be aware of the laws and regulations of the various localities in which the organization operates and should take actions that are consistent with those legal requirements. The internal auditor should consider obtaining legal advice if he or she is uncertain of the applicable legal requirements.

9. Many professional associations hold their members to a duty to disclose illegal or unethical activities. The distinguishing mark of a "profession" is its acceptance of broad responsibilities to the public and its protection of the general welfare. In addition to examining the legal requirements, IIA members and all Certified Internal Auditors should follow the requirements outlined in The IIA's Code of Ethics concerning illegal or unethical acts.

Internal Auditor's Decision

10. An internal auditor has a professional duty and an ethical responsibility to evaluate carefully all the evidence and the reasonableness of his or her conclusions and decide whether further actions may be needed to protect the interests of the organization, its stakeholders, the outside community, or the institutions of society. Also, the auditor will need to consider the duty of confidentiality imposed by The IIA's Code of Ethics to respect the value and ownership of information and avoid disclosing it without appropriate authority, unless there is a legal or professional obligation to do so. In this evaluation process, the auditor should seek the advice of legal counsel and, if appropriate, other experts. Those discussions may be helpful in providing a different perspective on the circumstances as well as offering opinions about the potential impact and consequences

of various possible actions. The manner in which the internal auditor seeks to resolve this type of complex and sensitive situation may create reprisals and potential liability.

11. Ultimately, the internal auditor must make a personal decision. The decision to communicate outside the normal chain of command should be based on a well-informed opinion that the wrongdoing is supported by substantial, credible evidence and that a legal or regulatory imperative or a professional or ethical obligation requires further action. The auditor's motive for acting should be the desire to stop the wrongful, harmful, or improper activity.

Practice Advisory 2500-1:
Monitoring Progress

Interpretation of *Standard 2500* from the
International Standards for the
Professional Practice of Internal Auditing

> *Related Standard*
> **2500 – Monitoring Progress**
> The chief audit executive should establish and maintain a system to monitor the disposition of results communicated to management.

Nature of this Practice Advisory: Internal auditors should consider the following suggestions when monitoring progress on results communicated to management. This guidance is not intended to represent all the considerations that may be necessary, but simply a recommended set of items that should be addressed.

1. The chief audit executive (CAE) should establish procedures to include:
    *   A time frame within which management's response to the engagement observations and recommendations is required.
    *   An evaluation of management's response.
    *   A verification of the response (if appropriate).
    *   A follow-up engagement (if appropriate).
    *   A communications procedure that escalates unsatisfactory responses/actions, including the assumption of risk, to the appropriate levels of management.

2. Certain reported observations and recommendations may be so significant as to require immediate action by management. These conditions should be monitored by the internal audit activity until corrected because of the effect they may have on the organization.

3. Techniques used to effectively monitor progress include:
    - Addressing engagement observations and recommendations to the appropriate levels of management responsible for taking corrective action.
    - Receiving and evaluating management responses to engagement observations and recommendations during the engagement or within a reasonable time period after the engagement results are communicated. Responses are more useful if they include sufficient information for the CAE to evaluate the adequacy and timeliness of corrective action.
    - Receiving periodic updates from management in order to evaluate the status of management's efforts to correct previously communicated conditions.
    - Receiving and evaluating information from other organizational units assigned responsibility for procedures of a follow-up or corrective nature.
    - Reporting to senior management or the board on the status of responses to engagement observations and recommendations.

Practice Advisory 2500.A1-1: Follow-up Process

Interpretation of *Standard 2500* from the *International Standards for the Professional Practice of Internal Auditing*

> ### Related Standard
> **2500.A1** – The chief audit executive should establish a follow-up process to monitor and ensure that management actions have been effectively implemented or that senior management has accepted the risk of not taking action.

Nature of this Practice Advisory: Internal auditors should consider the following suggestions when establishing follow-up processes. This guidance is not intended to represent all the considerations that may be necessary during such an evaluation, but simply a recommended set of items that should be addressed.

1. Internal auditors should determine that corrective action was taken and is achieving the desired results, or that senior management or the board has assumed the risk of not taking corrective action on reported observations.

2. Follow-up by internal auditors is defined as a process by which they determine the adequacy, effectiveness, and timeliness of actions taken by management on reported engagement observations and recommendations, including those made by external auditors and others.

3. Responsibility for follow-up should be defined in the internal audit activity's written charter. The nature, timing, and extent of follow-up should be determined by the chief audit executive (CAE). Factors that should be considered in determining appropriate follow-up procedures are:

    - The significance of the reported observation or recommendation.
    - The degree of effort and cost needed to correct the reported condition.
    - The impact that may result should the corrective action fail.
    - The complexity of the corrective action.
    - The time period involved.

4. There may also be instances where the CAE judges that management's oral or written response shows that action already taken is sufficient when weighed against the relative importance of the engagement observation or recommendation. On such occasions, follow-up may be performed as part of the next engagement.

5. Internal auditors should ascertain that actions taken on engagement observations and recommendations remedy the underlying conditions.

6. The CAE is responsible for scheduling follow-up activities as part of developing engagement work schedules. Scheduling of follow-up should be based on the risk and exposure involved, as well as the degree of difficulty and the significance of timing in implementing corrective action.

Practice Advisory 2600-1: Management's Acceptance of Risks

**Interpretation of *Standard 2600* from the
*International Standards for the
Professional Practice of Internal Auditing***

Related Standard
2600 – Management's Acceptance of Risks
When the chief audit executive believes that senior management has accepted a level of residual risk that is unacceptable to the organization, the chief audit executive should discuss the matter with senior management. If the decision regarding residual risk is not resolved, the chief audit executive and senior management should report the matter to the board for resolution.

Nature of this Practice Advisory: Internal auditors should consider the following suggestions involving management's acceptance of risks. This guidance is not intended to represent all the considerations that may be necessary, but simply a recommended set of items that should be addressed.

1. Management is responsible for deciding the appropriate action to be taken in response to reported engagement observations and recommendations. The chief audit executive is responsible for assessing such management action for the timely resolution of the matters reported as engagement observations and recommendations. In deciding the extent of follow-up, internal auditors should consider procedures of a follow-up nature performed by others in the organization.

2. As stated in Section 2060 of the *International Standards for the Professional Practice of Internal Auditing (Standards)*, paragraph 3 of Practice Advisory 2060-1, senior management may decide to assume the risk of not correcting the reported condition because of cost or other considerations. The board should be informed of senior management's decision on all significant engagement observations and recommendations.

TRANSLATION OR ADAPTATION OF THE PROFESSIONAL PRACTICES FRAMEWORK AND ITS RELATED GUIDANCE

(Administrative Directive No. 2)

Purpose

This section describes the administrative procedures for adapting the Professional Practices Framework and Framework-related Guidance to audit environments throughout the world and/or for translating them into languages other than English.

Legal Basis

The Professional Practices Framework and the related Guidance of The Institute of Internal Auditors (IIA) are copyrighted by The Institute of Internal Auditors, 247 Maitland Avenue, Altamonte Springs, Florida 32701-4201, USA, whether separately published or published in any of The IIA's publications. All rights reserved.

Under copyright laws and agreements, no part of any of the Framework and related Guidance may be reproduced, stored in a retrieval system, or translated in any form by any means — electronic, mechanical, photocopying, recording, or otherwise — without prior written permission of The IIA. Except as provided by separate agreement, permission to adapt or translate the Framework and related Guidance is granted solely by The IIA. Distribution of approved adaptations or translations are to be made under the direction of IIA affiliates.

Translation

Translation of The IIA's Framework and related Guidance into languages other than English is necessary to provide the same level of guidance to all members of The IIA and all IIA affiliates. Permission should be obtained from The IIA before any translations are initiated in order to obtain appropriate guidance and, where translations have already been approved, to avoid having unnecessary variations in the translations into any one language.

The IIA encourages IIA affiliates where English is not the primary language to furnish translations of The IIA's Framework and related Guidance to their members, provided that:

1. The translation is in a form as close as possible to, and preserves the concepts of, the original;

2. Copies of the translated documents are submitted to The IIA, and are accompanied by a statement signed by the president of the IIA affiliate and by a qualified translator, attesting that the meanings and concepts of the original have been preserved.

3. Permission is obtained from The IIA before the translation is published.

4. To provide a minimum level of guidance, the translated Framework and related Guidance should include the Definition of Internal Auditing, Code of Ethics, *International Standards for the Professional Practice of Internal Auditing* – Attribute

Standards, *International Standards for the Professional Practice of Internal Auditing* – Performance Standards, and the *International Standards for the Professional Practice of Internal Auditing* – Implementation Standards.

5. The translated version includes a translated statement that "Permission has been obtained from the copyright holder, The Institute of Internal Auditors, 247 Maitland Avenue, Altamonte Springs, Florida 32701-4201, USA, to publish this translation, which is the same as the original in all material respects as the original."

Adaptation

Laws, regulations, and customs of different countries may require that specific Guidance be adapted for use in the audit environments of such countries. Before publication of adapted Guidance to their members, IIA affiliates are required to:

1. Apply to The IIA for approval of the adaptation, indicating the nature of any modifications, the reasons they are required, and the effect on the professional practice of internal auditing in the country, if such modifications are not made.

2. Provide copies of the adapted and, where appropriate, translated documents to The IIA, with an accompanying a statement attesting that, to the extent they are applicable to the local environment, the concepts contained in the original document have been preserved in the adaptation. Attestation statements must be signed by the president of the IIA affiliate and, for translated documents, by a qualified translator.

3. Include in all adapted versions the statement that "Permission has been obtained from the copyright holder, The Institute of Internal Auditors, 247 Maitland Avenue, Altamonte Springs,

Florida 32701-4201, USA, to publish this adaptation of the original for use in [name of country]. The concepts enunciated in the original have been preserved in this adapted version."

Proposing Changes or Additions to Guidance

Nothing in this statement should preclude an IIA affiliate from proposing changes or additions to any of The IIA's Guidance. Suggestions of this nature should be directed to the chairman of the Internal Auditing Standards Board.